Opa Application Development

A rapid and secure web development framework
to develop web applications quickly and easily in Opa

Li Wenbo

BIRMINGHAM - MUMBAI

Opa Application Development

First published: June 2013

Production Reference: 1040613

Published by Packt Publishing Ltd.
Livery Place
35 Livery Street
Birmingham B3 2PB, UK.

ISBN 978-1-78216-374-9

www.packtpub.com

Cover Image by Parag Kadam (paragvkadam@gmail.com)

Credits

Author
Li Wenbo

Reviewers
Joseph Goldman
Alok Menghrajani

Acquisition Editor
Mary Jasmine Nadar

Commissioning Editor
Neha Nagwekar

Technical Editors
Sharvari H. Baet
Priyanka Kalekar

Project Coordinator
Sherin Padayatty

Proofreader
Paul Hindle

Indexer
Hemangini Bari

Graphics
Abhinash Sahu

Production Coordinator
Aparna Bhagat

Cover Work
Aparna Bhagat

About the Author

Li Wenbo studied Computer Science and Technology at Wuhan University, graduating with a master's degree. He has two years experience working as a Software Engineer in a leading telecom company in China. He has been doing web development for about 8 years, ever since he was a student at Wuhan University. He is familiar with a lot of programming languages such as C/C++, Java, JavaScript, PHP, and so on, and he has a passion for new things and technologies. Li tried the Opa framework last year and found it very interesting. He then participated in an Opa challenge and won the first prize.

Li Wenbo is now a freelance developer and owns a small studio in Wuhan, China.

About the Reviewers

Joseph Goldman is an experienced freelance programmer who cut his teeth on 8086 Assembler before joining the Homo Sapiens race by learning to walk upright and adopting more conversational and universal programming languages such as C, Objective C, Smalltalk, Pascal, and more. Over his illustrious 30 year career, he has programmed for VAX under VMS, Sun Microsystems work stations, MS DOS 8088 - Pentium CPUs, MS Windows, Mac OSX, and Linux. A tireless early adopter of new programming paradigms and languages, he is very fond of the new generation of functional and object-oriented programming languages, such as Google's Dart, Opa, Scala, and more, as well as other innovative language designs, most notably REBOL. Today, he specializes in writing web apps and mobile apps for iOS and Android platforms, both smart phones as well as tablets. He is self-employed and can be reached at TheAppsDude@gmail.com. In the late 1990s, Mr. Goldman co-authored *REBOL - The Official Guide* that was published in the year 2000 by Osborne McGraw-Hill.

Alok Menghrajani Computer Science at EPFL and CMU. He graduated in 2005. He then started working in the field of web security and is currently an engineer at Facebook.

Alok got the opportunity to learn Opa when it was open sourced. He realized the potential this framework offered to improve web development; Opa helps build web applications faster and in a safer way.

He has made various contributions to Opa: reporting bugs, providing feedback to the core team, and helping out with community events such as hackathons.

He is also the author of http://pixlpaste.com/, a web application to share screenshots and images written in Opa.

He has also worked on *Opa: Up and Running* and *JavaScript for PHP Developers*.

www.PacktPub.com

Support files, eBooks, discount offers and more

You might want to visit www.PacktPub.com for support files and downloads related to your book.

Did you know that Packt offers eBook versions of every book published, with PDF and ePub files available? You can upgrade to the eBook version at www.PacktPub.com and as a print book customer, you are entitled to a discount on the eBook copy. Get in touch with us at service@packtpub.com for more details.

At www.PacktPub.com, you can also read a collection of free technical articles, sign up for a range of free newsletters and receive exclusive discounts and offers on Packt books and eBooks.

http://PacktLib.PacktPub.com

Do you need instant solutions to your IT questions? PacktLib is Packt's online digital book library. Here, you can access, read and search across Packt's entire library of books.

Why Subscribe?

- Fully searchable across every book published by Packt
- Copy and paste, print and bookmark content
- On demand and accessible via web browser

Free Access for Packt account holders

If you have an account with Packt at www.PacktPub.com, you can use this to access PacktLib today and view nine entirely free books. Simply use your login credentials for immediate access.

Table of Contents

Preface

Opa Application Development dives into all the concepts and components required to build a web application with Opa. The first half of this book shows the basic building blocks that you will need to develop an Opa application, including the syntax of Opa, web development aspects, client and server communication, as well as slicing, plugins, databases, and so on.

Opa is a full-stack open source web development framework for JavaScript that lets you write secure and scalable web applications. It generates the standard Node. js and MongoDB applications, natively supports HTML5 and CSS, and automates many aspects of modern web application programming. It handles all aspects of web programming written in one consistent language and is compiled to web standards.

This book is a practical, hands-on guide that provides you with a number of step-by-step exercises. It covers almost all the aspects of developing a web application with Opa, which will help you take advantage of the real power of Opa to build secure and powerful web applications rapidly.

What this book covers

Chapter 1, Getting Started with Opa, introduces how to install and set up an Opa development environment.

*Chapter 2, Basic Synt*ax, covers the basic syntax of Opa.

Chapter 3, Developing Web Applications, introduces the fundamental knowledge about developing a web application with Opa.

Chapter 4, Using Bootstrap, introduces how to use Bootstrap in Opa when developing a web application.

*Chapter 5, Communicating Between Client and Se*rver, covers client and server slicing and communicating.

Chapter 6, Binding with Other Languages, explains how to bind JavaScript and Node.js to Opa.

Chapter 7, Working with Databases, explains everything about storing, updating, and querying data in a database with MongoDB as a backend.

Chapter 8, Internationalization, introduces the internationalization approach of Opa.

Chapter 9, Building a Chat Application, explains how to build a web chat application with Opa.

Chapter 10, Building a Game – Pacman, explains how to handle image and audio using a canvas when building a Pacman game.

Chapter 11, Building a Social Mobile Application – LiveRoom, explains how to build a social mobile application with Opa.

What you need for this book

Required knowledge for this book is as follows:

- Basic knowledge about HTML and CSS
- Basic knowledge about JavaScript
- Some programming experience

Software required for this book is as follows:

- Node.js (`http://www.nodejs.org/`)
- The Opa framework (`http://opalang.org/`)
- MongoDB (`http://www.mongodb.org/`)
- A text editor tool, SublimeText (`http://www.sublimetext.com/`) is recommended.

Who this book is for

This book is written for web developers who want to get started with the Opa framework and who want to build web applications with it. Web development experience is assumed and would be helpful for understanding this book.

Conventions

In this book, you will find a number of styles of text that distinguish between different kinds of information. Here are some examples of these styles, and an explanation of their meaning.

Code words in text are shown as follows: "We can include other contexts through the use of the `include` directive."

A block of code is set as follows:

```
type Student = {string name, int age, float score}
Student stu = { name:"li", age:28, score:80.0}
```

When we wish to draw your attention to a particular part of a code block, the relevant lines or items are set in bold:

```
type Student = {string name, int age, float score}
Student stu = { name:"li", age:28, score:80.0}
```

New terms and **important words** are shown in bold. Words that you see on the screen, in menus or dialog boxes for example, appear in the text like this: "Clicking on the **Next** button moves you to the next screen".

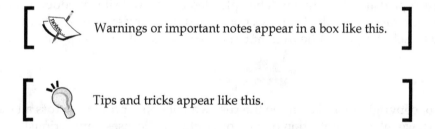

> Warnings or important notes appear in a box like this.

> Tips and tricks appear like this.

Reader feedback

Feedback from our readers is always welcome. Let us know what you think about this book—what you liked or may have disliked. Reader feedback is important for us to develop titles that you really get the most out of.

To send us general feedback, simply send an e-mail to feedback@packtpub.com, and mention the book title via the subject of your message.

If there is a topic that you have expertise in and you are interested in either writing or contributing to a book, see our author guide on www.packtpub.com/authors.

Customer support

Now that you are the proud owner of a Packt book, we have a number of things to help you to get the most from your purchase.

Downloading the example code

You can download the example code files for all Packt books you have purchased from your account at `http://www.packtpub.com`. If you purchased this book elsewhere, you can visit `http://www.packtpub.com/support` and register to have the files e-mailed directly to you.

Errata

Although we have taken every care to ensure the accuracy of our content, mistakes do happen. If you find a mistake in one of our books — maybe a mistake in the text or the code — we would be grateful if you would report this to us. By doing so, you can save other readers from frustration and help us improve subsequent versions of this book. If you find any errata, please report them by visiting `http://www.packtpub.com/submit-errata`, selecting your book, clicking on the **errata submission form** link, and entering the details of your errata. Once your errata are verified, your submission will be accepted and the errata will be uploaded on our website, or added to any list of existing errata, under the Errata section of that title. Any existing errata can be viewed by selecting your title from `http://www.packtpub.com/support`.

Piracy

Piracy of copyright material on the Internet is an ongoing problem across all media. At Packt, we take the protection of our copyright and licenses very seriously. If you come across any illegal copies of our works, in any form, on the Internet, please provide us with the location address or website name immediately so that we can pursue a remedy.

Please contact us at `copyright@packtpub.com` with a link to the suspected pirated material.

We appreciate your help in protecting our authors, and our ability to bring you valuable content.

Questions

You can contact us at `questions@packtpub.com` if you are having a problem with any aspect of the book, and we will do our best to address it.

1
Getting Started with Opa

This chapter shows how to install Opa and set its environment. A simple Opa program will also be shown to give a first glimpse of Opa programming.

Installing Opa

This section is about installation and configuration of Opa. You can get a more detailed installation guide that includes how to build Opa from source on Opa's webpage (`https://github.com/MLstate/opalang/wiki/Getting-started`). This section will give us brief instructions on how to install Opa compiler, Node.js, and some required modules for Node.js.

Installing Node.js

Node.js (`http://nodejs.org`) is a platform for building fast and scalable network applications. It is the backend of Opa (since Opa 1.0.0). We need to install Node.js first before installing Opa. The following are the steps to install Node.js on various operating systems:

- **Mac OS**: Following are the steps to install Node.js:
    1. Download the latest `.pkg` package from `http://nodejs.org/dist/latest/`.
    2. Double-click on the package to install Node.js.

- **Ubuntu and Debian Linux**: To install Node.js on Ubuntu and Debian Linux, type the following commands:
    ```
    $sudo apt-get install python-software-properties
    $sudo add-apt-repository ppa:chris-lea/node.js
    $sudo apt-get update
    $sudo apt-get install nodejs npm
    ```

Downloading the example code files

You can download the example code files for all Packt books you have purchased from your account at http://www.packtpub.com. If you purchased this book elsewhere, you can visit http://www.packtpub.com/support and register to have the files e-mailed directly to you.

- **Windows**: The following are the steps to install Node.js:

    1. Download the latest .msi package from http://nodejs.org/dist/latest/.
    2. Double-click on the package to install Node.js on Windows.

Type the following commands to confirm your installation. If everything goes right, you will see the version information of Node.js and npm.

```
$ node -v
$ npm -v
```

Installing the required modules

There are several modules that are required by Opa to run an application. Type the following command to install these modules:

```
$ npm install -g mongodb formidable nodemailer simplesmtp imap
```

Installing the Opa compiler

The easiest solution for installing Opa is to download an installer from the Opa website (http://opalang.org/). You can also get the installer from Opa's GitHub repository (https://github.com/MLstate/opalang/downloads). At the time this book is being written, the latest version of Opa is 1.1.0.

Following are the steps to install Opa on various operating systems:

- **Mac OS X**: Download the latest .dmg package and double-click on it to install. You will need the password of an administrative account.
- **Ubuntu and Debian Linux**: Download the latest .deb package and double-click on it to install. You can also install it with the following command line:

    ```
    $sudo dpkg -i opa-1.1.0.x86.deb
    ```

- **Windows**: Download the latest `.exe` file and double-click on it to install. Note that only 64-bit packages are available for Windows at this time.

- **Other Linux**: To install Opa follow these steps:

  1. Download the latest `.run` package for Linux.

  2. Go to the download folder and add an execution privilege to the downloaded file by running the following command:

     ```
     $ chmod a+x opa-1.1.0.x64.run
     ```

  3. Run the installing script:

     ```
     $ sudo ./opa-1.1.0.x64.run
     ```

Testing the installation

To test if Opa is installed properly on your computer, run the following command:

```
$ opa --version
```

Opa is installed properly if the version information of the Opa compiler is printed.

Setting up editors

You can write Opa codes with any text editor you like, but a good editor can make coding easier. This section is about setting up editors you may commonly use. For now, Sublime Text is the most complete **Integrated Development Environment (IDE)** for Opa.

Sublime Text

Sublime Text (`http://www.sublimetext.com/`) is a sophisticated text editor for code, markup, and prose. You can download and try Sublime Text for free from `http://www.sublimetext.com/2`.

There is an Opa plugin that offers syntax highlighting, code completion, and some other features. To install the plugin, follow these steps:

1. Get the plugin from `https://github.com/downloads/MLstate/OpaSublimeText/Opa.sublime-package`.

2. Move it to `~/.config/sublime-text2/Installed Packages/` (in Linux), or `%%APPDATA%%\Sublime Text 2\Installed Packages\` (in Windows), or `~/Library/Application Support/Sublime Text 2/Installed Packages` (in Mac).

3. Start Sublime and check if the menu entry (**View** | **Syntax** | **Opa**) is present. If everything goes well, the file with the .opa extension should automatically have its syntax highlighted. If not, please make sure you are using the Opa plugin (**View** | **Syntax** | **Opa**). We can navigate to **Edit** | **Line** | **Reindent** to auto-indent the Opa code.

Vim

Vim (http://www.vim.org/) is a highly configurable text editor, freely available for many different platforms. The Opa installation package provides a mode for Vim at /usr/share/opa/vim/ (for Linux) or /opt/mlstate/share/opa/vim/ (for Mac OS). To enable Vim to detect Opa syntax, copy these files to your .vim directory in your home folder (create it if it does not exist already):

- On Linux, type the following command:

```
$cp -p /usr/share/opa/vim/* ~/.vim/
```

- On Mac OS, type the following command:

```
$cp -p /opt/mlstate/share/opa/vim/* ~/.vim
```

Emacs

On Mac OS X, you can either use Aquamacs and the package installation will take care of it, or you should add the following line to your configuration file (which might be ~/.emacs; create it if it does not exist already):

```
(autoload 'opa-classic-mode "/Library/Application Support/Emacs/
site-lisp/opa-mode/opa-mode.el" "Opa CLASSIC editing mode." t)
(autoload 'opa-js-mode "/Library/Application Support/Emacs/
site-lisp/opa-mode/opa-js-mode.el" "Opa JS editing mode." t)
(add-to-list 'auto-mode-alist '("\.opa$" . opa-js-mode))
(add-to-list 'auto-mode-alist '("\.js\.opa$" . opa-js-mode))
(add-to-list 'auto-mode-alist '("\.classic\.opa$" . opa-classic-
mode))
```

On Linux, add the following lines to your configuration file:

```
(autoload 'opa-js-mode "/usr/share/opa/emacs/opa-js-mode.el" "Opa
JS editing mode." t)
(autoload 'opa-classic-mode "/usr/share/opa/emacs/opa-mode.el"
"Opa CLASSIC editing mode." t)
(add-to-list 'auto-mode-alist '("\.opa$" . opa-js-mode))
(add-to-list 'auto-mode-alist '("\.js\.opa$" . opa-js-mode))
(add-to-list 'auto-mode-alist '("\.classic\.opa$" . opa-classic-
mode))
```

For Eclipse, the experimental plugin is available at `https://github.com/MLstate/opa-eclipse-plugin`.

Your first Opa application

As a first example, here is the most simple program in Opa:

```
jlog("hello Opa!")
```

Compile and run it:

```
$ opa hello.opa -o hello.js
$ ./hello.js
```

 We can type `opa hello.opa --` to compile and run the code in a single line.

The code does nothing but prints **hello Opa** on your screen. If you can see this message, it means Opa is working properly on your machine.

Summary

In this chapter, we learned how to install Opa, set up a proper editor, and write our first Opa program. In the next chapter, we will have a brief look at the basic grammar of the Opa language.

2
Basic Syntax

In this chapter, we will introduce the basic syntax of Opa. This chapter will not cover every little tiny thing about Opa, but it is something you should know. It's also assumed that you have some basic knowledge about computer programming.

Basic datatypes

Datatypes are the shapes of data manipulated by an application. Opa uses datatypes to perform sanity and security checks on your application. Opa also uses datatypes to perform a number of optimizations. There are three basic datatypes in Opa: integers, floats, and strings. Also, you can define your type with the keyword `type`:

```
type Student = {string name, int age, float score}
Student stu = { name:"li", age:28, score:80.0}
```

Actually, thanks to a mechanism of type inference, Opa can work in most cases even if you do not provide any type information. For example:

```
x = 10        // the same as: int x = 10
x = {a:1,b:2} // the type of x is: {a:int, b:int}
```

So in the rest of this chapter, we will not address type information before variable, but you should know what type it is in your mind. In actual coding, a best practice is to provide the datatypes of our main functions and to let the inference engine pick up the datatypes of all the local variables and minor functions.

Integers

It is quite simple to write integer literals; there are a number of ways to do so:

```
x = 10     // 10 in base 10
x = 0xA    // 10 in base 16, any case works (0Xa, 0XA, 0xa)
x = 0o12   // 10 in base 8
x = 0b1010 // 10 in base 2
```

The tailing semicolon is optional in Opa; you can add it if you want.

Opa provides the module `Int` (`http://doc.opalang.org/module/stdlib.core/Int`) to operate on integers. The following are the most used functions:

```
i1 = Int.abs(-10)        // i1 = 10
i2 = Int.max(10,8)       // i2 = 10
```

There is no automatic type conversion between `float`, `int`, and `String`. So, use the following functions to convert between `int`, `float`, and `String`.

```
i3 = Int.of_float(10.6)      // i3 = 10
i4 = Int.of_string("0xA")    // i4 = 10, 0xA is 10 in dec
f1 = Int.to_float(10)        // f1 = 10.0, f1 is a float
s1 = Int.to_string(10)       // s1 = "10", s1 is a string
```

Floats

It is also easy to define floats. They can be written in the following ways:

```
x = 12.21    // the normal one
x = .12      // omitting the leading zero
x = 12.      // to indicate this is a float, not an integer
x = 12.5e10  // scientific notation
```

Opa provides the module `Float` (`http://doc.opalang.org/module/stdlib.core/Float`) to operate on floats. The following are the most used functions:

```
f1 = Float.abs(-10.0)        //f1 = 10.0
f2 = Float.ceil(10.5)        //f2 = 11.0
f3 = Float.floor(10.5)        //f3 = 10.0
f4 = Float.round(10.5)       //f4 = 11.0
f5 = Float.of_int(10)        //f5 = 10.0
f6 = Float.of_string("10.5") //f6 = 10.5
i1 = Float.to_int(10.5)      //i1 = 10, i1 is an integer
s1 = Float.to_string(10.5)   //s1 = "10.5", s1 is a string
```

Strings

In Opa, text is represented by immutable utf8-encoded character strings. String literals follow roughly the same syntax used in C language, Java, or JavaScript. Note that you will have to escape special characters with backslashes.

```
x = "hello!"
x = "\"" // special characters can be escaped with backslashes
```

Opa has a feature called string insertions, which can put arbitrary expressions into a string. You can do that by embedding an expression between curly braces into a string. For example:

```
x = "1 + 2 = {1+2}"    //will produce "1 + 2 = 3"
lang = "Opa"
y = "I love {lang}!"   //will produce "I love Opa!"
```

Opa provides the module String (http://doc.opalang.org/module/stdlib. core/String) to operate on strings. The most commonly used are as follows:

```
s = "I love Opa! "               //Note there is a space at the end.
len = String.length(s)           //get length, len = 12
isEmpty = String.is_empty(s)     //test if a string is empty, false
isBlank = String.is_blank(s)     //test if a string is blank, false
cont = String.contains(s,"Opa")  //check if a string contains a
                                 //substring,true
idx1 = String.index("love",s)    //found, idx1 = {some:2}
idx2 = String.index("loving",s)  //not found, idx2 = {none}
ch = String.get(0,s)             //get nth char, ch = 'I'
s2 = String.trim(s)              //do trim, s2 = "I love Opa!"
s3 = String.replace("I","We",s2) //s3 = "We love Opa!"
```

Sum

A value has a sum type t or u, meaning that the values of this type are either of the two variants, a value of type t or a value of type u.

A good example of sum type are Boolean values, which are defined as follows:

```
type bool = {true} or {false}
```

Thus, a variable of type bool can be either {true} or {false}. Another commonly used sum type is the option type, which is defined as:

```
type option('a) = {none} or {'a some}
```

The option(`a) value is either none or some (a value x of type `a). Type `a means any type. This is a type-safe way to deal with possibly non-existing values. The option type is widely used; let's take String.index for example:

```
idx1 = String.index("love","I love Opa!")    //idx1 = {some:2}
idx2 = String.index("loving","I love Opa!")  //idx2 = {none}
```

The return type of `String.index` is the option (`int`), which means it will return a {`some:int`} record if a substring appears or a {`none`} record if it doesn't.

Note that the sum datatypes are not limited to two cases; they can have tens of cases.

Functions

Opa is a functional language. One of its features is that functions are regular values, which means a function may be passed as a parameter or returned as a result. As such, they follow the same naming rules as any other value.

```
function f(x,y){        // function f with the two parameters x and y
  x + y + 1
}
function int f(x,y){  // explicitly indicates the return type
  x + y + 1
}
```

Last expression return

You may notice that there is no return inside the body of a function. That's because Opa uses last expression return, which means the last expression of a function is the return value. For example:

```
function max(x,y){
   if(x >= y) x else y
}
```

If x is greater than or equal to y, then x is the last expression and x will be returned; if y is greater than x, then y is the last expression and y will be returned.

Modules

Functionalities are usually regrouped into modules; for example:

```
module  M {
  x = 1
  y = x
  function test(){ jlog("testing") }
}
```

We can access the content of a module by using the dot operator (`.`); for instance, `M.x`, `M.y`, and `M.test`. Actually, the content of a module is not field definitions, but bindings. In this example, we bind integer 1 to variable x, and bind the value of variable x to variable y.

Data structures

The only way to build data structures in Opa is to use records, which we will talk about later on. All other data structures, such as tuples and lists, are based on records. Opa provides different modules to help the user to manipulate lists and maps. Let's first have a look at records.

Records

Simply speaking, a record is a collection of data. Here is how to build a record:

```
x = {} // the empty record
x = {a:2,b:3} //a record with field "a" and "b"
```

The empty record,{ }, has a synonym, void, which means the same thing. There are a number of syntactic shortcuts available to write records concisely. First, if you give a field name without the field value, it means the value of this field is void:

```
x = {a}        // means {a:void}
x = {a, b:2} // means {a:void b:2}
```

The second shorthand we always use is the sign ~. It means if the field value is left empty, assign it with a variable having the same name as the field name:

```
x = {~a, b:2}    // means {a:a, b:2}
x = ~{a, b}       // means {a:a, b:b}
x = ~{a, b, c:4} // means {a:a, b:b, c:4}
x = ~{a:{b}, c}  // means {a:{b:void}, c:c}, NOT {a:{b:b}, c:c}
//Consider this more meaningful example
name = "Li"; sex  = "Male"; age  = 28;
person = ~{name, sex, age} //means {name:"Li", sex:"Male", age: 28}
```

We can also build a record deriving from an existing record using the keyword with:

```
x = {a:1,b:2,c:3}
y = {x with a:"1",b:5} // y = {a:"1", b:5, c:3}
```

Note that you can redefine as many fields as you want. In the example we saw just now, the field a in y is a string, but the field a in x is an integer. Here are some more examples about deriving:

```
X = {a:1, b:{c:"2", d:3.0}}
// you can update fields deep in the record
y = {x with b.c:"200"}  // y = {a:1, b:{c:"200", d:3.0}}
// you can use the same syntactic shortcuts as used before
y = {x with a}           // means {x with a:void}
y = {x with ~a}          // means {x with a:a}
y = ~{x with a, b:{e}}   // means {x with a:a, b:{e}}
```

Tuples

An N-tuple is a sequence of *n* elements, where N is a positive integer. In Opa, an N-tuple is just a record with fields f1 to fN:

```
x = (1,)            // a tuple of size 1, the same as {f1:1}
x = (1,"2",{a:3}) // a size 3 tuple, the same as {f1:1, f2:"2",
f3:{a:3}}
y = {x with f1:2} // we can manipulate a tuple the same way as a
                      //record
// y = {f1:2, f2:"2", f3:{a:3}}
```

Note the trailing comma in the first case; it differentiates a 1-tuple from a parenthesized expression. The trailing comma is allowed for any other tuple, although, it makes no difference whether you write it or not in these cases.

Lists

In Opa, a list (linked list) is an immutable data structure, meant to contain finite or infinite sets of elements of the same type. Actually, list is just a record with special structures, which is defined as:

```
type list('a) = {nil} or {'a hd, list('a) tl}
```

Here is how to build lists:

```
x = []        // the empty list, equals to {nil}
x = [2,3,4] // a three element list, the same as a record:
              // {hd:2, tl:{hd:3, tl:{hd:4, tl:{nil}}}}
y = [0,1|x] // this will put 0,1 on top of x: [0,1,2,3,4]
```

Lists in Opa are much like arrays in C language and Java. But there are differences. First, lists are immutable in Opa, which means elements of a list cannot be changed by assignment. Second, the way we manipulate lists are different. We use the module List (http://doc.opalang.org/module/stdlib.core/List) to manage lists in Opa. The following are the most commonly used operations on lists (which will be explained in the subsequent sections):

```
l = [1,2,3]
len = List.length(l)      // return the length of a list
isEmpty = List.is_empty(l) // test if a list is empty
head = List.head(l)        // get the first element, will fail if
                            // the list is empty
element = List.get(0,l)    // get nth element, return option('a)
l1 = List.add(4,l)         // adding an element at the head of a
                            //list
```

```
12 = 4 +> 1              // a shortcut for List.add
13 = List.remove(3,1)    // removing an element
14 = List.drop(2,1)      // drop the first n elements
```

Iterating through a list

In C language or Java, we use a `for` or a `while` loop to iterate through lists or arrays. They look something like this:

```
int[] numbers = [1,2,3,4,5]
for(int i=0; i<numbers.length; i++){ //do something }
```

But in Opa, it is totally different. To loop through a list, we use `List.fold` or `List.foldi`. `List.fold` is a powerful function that you can use to do almost anything you want on a list. Here is a simple example of getting the length of a list:

```
len = List.fold(function(_,i){ i+1 }, ["a","b","c"], 0)
```

`List.fold` takes three parameters. The first is a function, the second is the list, and the third is an initial value. It loops through the list and applies the function on each element. So, if we name the function `f`, it is executed something like this:

```
len = f("c", f("b", f("a",0)))
```

First, `f("a",0)` will be executed and will return 1, here 0 is the initial value and `a` is the first element. Then `f("b",1)` will return 2 and at last `f("c",2)` will return 3. Here is a little more complicated example:

```
//find the max natural number in the list
max = List.fold(function(x,a){
  if(x > a) x else a
},[1,4,3,2,7,8,5],0)
```

Finding elements

We have many ways to find an element in a list. `List.index` searches the first occurrence of an element and returns its index. `List.index_p` searches the first occurrence of any element matching a given function and returns its index. `List.find` is the same as `List.index_p`, but returns the element itself but not its index. For example:

```
l = ["a","b","c"]
r1 = List.index("b",l)                      // r1 = {some:1}
r2 = List.index("x",l)                      // r2 = {none}
r3 = List.index_p(function(x){ x == "b"},l) // r3 = {some:1}
r4 = List.find(function(x){ x == "b"},l)    // r4 = {some:"b"}
```

Transforming lists

If you want to project elements to a new list, for example doubling the number in a list or selecting the odd numbers, you can do this with `List.map` and `List.filter`. Here are some examples:

```
l1 = [1,2,3,4,5]
l2 = List.map(function(x){ 2*x }, l1); //l2 = [2,4,6,8,10]
l3 = List.filter(function(x){mod(x,2) == 0},l1); // l3 = [2,4]
```

Sorting a list

Call the function `List.sort` to sort a list in the usual order. The usual order means the default order, that is, numbers from small to big and strings in alphabetical order. Consider the following code:

```
l1 = List.sort(["by","as","of","At"]) //l1 = ["At","as","by","of"]
l2 = List.sort([1,3,4,6,2])           //l2 = [1,2,3,4,6]
```

`List.sort_by` uses the usual order, but it projects elements, for example, converting strings to lower-case before comparing them. `List.sort_with` allows us to use our own comparing function.

To make that clear, suppose there are three points, P1 (1, 3), P2 (3, 2), and P3 (2, 1), and we want to sort them in two different ways:

- By their Y coordinates
- By distance from the origin of the coordinates (0, 0)

Let's see how to do that in Opa:

```
p = [{x:1,y:3},{x:3,y:2},{x:2,y:1}]
l1 = List.sort_with(function(p1,p2){  // sort by Y corordination
  if(p1.y >= p2.y) {gt} else {lt}
},p)
l2 = List.sort_by(function(p){        //sort by distance
  p.x*p.x + p.y*p.y
},p)
```

Maps

Maps are an important data structure just like lists. The most common cases of maps in Opa are `stringmap` and `intmap`. `stringmap` is a map from string to value of some type, while `intmap` is a map from numbers to value of some type.

The way we manipulate maps is almost the same as lists, it is unwise to repeat it again. Here are some of the most used operations:

```
m1 = Map.empty                    // create an empty map
m2 = StringMap.empty              // create an empty stringmap
m3 = IntMap.empty                 // create an empty intmap
m4 = Map.add("key1","val1",m1)    // adding a key-val pair
v1 = Map.get("key1",m4)           // getting a value
m5 = Map.remove("key1",m4)        // removing a key
```

Pattern matching

Pattern matching is a generalization of C language or Java's `switch` statement. In C language and Java, the `switch` statement only allows you to choose from many statements based on an integer (including `char`) or an `enum` value. While in Opa, pattern matching is more powerful than that. The more general syntax for pattern matching is:

```
match(<expr>){
case <case_1>: <expression_1>
case <case_2>: <expression_2>
case <case_n>: < expression_n>
}
```

When a pattern is executed, `<expr>` is evaluated to a value, which is then matched against each pattern in order until a case is found. You can think about it this way:

```
if (case_1 matched) expression_1 else {
  if (case_2 matched) expression_2 else {
    ...
        if (case_n matched) expression_n else no_matches
        ...
  }
}
```

The rules of pattern matching are simple and are as follows:

- **Rule 1**: Any value matches the pattern _
- **Rule 2**: Any value matches the variable pattern x, and the value is bound to the identifier x
- **Rule 3**: An integer/float/string matches an integer/float/string pattern when they are equal

- **Rule 4**: A record (including tuples and lists) matches a closed record pattern when both records have the same fields and the value of the fields matches the pattern component-wise

- **Rule 5**: A record (including tuples and lists) matches an open record pattern when the value has all the fields of the pattern (but can have more) and the value of the common fields matches the pattern component-wise

- **Rule 6**: A value matches a pattern as x pattern when the value matches the pattern, and additionally it binds x to the value

- **Rule 7**: A value matches an OR pattern if one of the values matches one of the two subpatterns

- **Rule 8**: In all the other cases, the matching fails

The first three and the last three rules (rule 1, 2, 3, 6, 7, 8) are easy to understand. Let's take a look at them:

```
match(y) {
case 0:        //if y == 0, match [rule 3]
case 1 as x:   //if y == 1, match and 1 is bound to x [rule 6]
case 2 | 3 :   //if y is 2 or 3, match [rule 7]
case x:        //any value will match and the value is bound
                 //to x [rule 2]
case _:        //match, we do not care about the value.
}
```

 This code will not compile, we just used it to illustrate the rules.

Rule 4 and rule 5 are a little more complicated. A close record pattern is a record with fixed fields. An open record pattern is a record that ends with ... to indicate that it may have other fields we do not care about. The following examples may make that clearer:

```
x = {a:1, b:2, c:3}
match(x) {
case {a:1,b:2}:     //a close record pattern, but will not match
//cause they do not have the same fields [rule 4]
case {a:1,b:2,c:2}: //a close record pattern, still will not match
//cause c is not equal [rule 4]
case {a:1,b:2,...}: //An open record pattern, matches [rule 5]
}
```

We can also match tuples and lists (since tuples and lists are special records, they are not hard to understand). For example:

```
t = (1,"2",3.0)
match(t){              //matching a tuple
case (1,"2",3.1): //not match, 3.1 != 3.0
case (1,"2",_):   //match, _ matches anything
case (1,"2",x):   //match, now x = 3.0
case {f1:1 ...}:  //match, remember tuples are just records
}
y = [1,2,3]
match(y){              //matching a list
case [1,2]:            //not match
case [1,2,_]:          //match, _ matches anything
case [1,2,x]:          //match, now x = 3
case [2,|_]:           //not match, '|_' means the rest of the list
case [1,|_]:           //match
case [1,2,|_]:         //match
case [1,x|_]:          //match, now x = 2
}
```

Text parsers

Parsing is something that web apps need to do quite often. Opa features a built-in syntax for building text parsers, which are first class values just as functions. The parser is based on parsing expression grammar (`http://en.wikipedia.org/wiki/Parsing_expression_grammar`), which may look like regular expressions at first, but do not behave anything like them. One big advantage of text parsers over regular expressions is that you can easily combine parsers. A good example is parsing URLs. Let's start right away with our first Opa parser:

```
first_parser = parser {
case "Opa"  : 1
}
```

For `first_parser`, the expressions are just literal strings, which means this parser will succeed only if fed with the string `"Opa"`. Then how to use this parser? The module `Parser` (`http://doc.opalang.org/module/stdlib.core.parser/Parser`) has a bunch of functions to deal with parsers. The most important one is:

```
Parser.try_parse : Parser.general_parser('a), string -> option('a)
```

It takes a parser and a string as parameters and produces an optional value of some type. Let's see how to use this function:

```
x = Parser.try_parse(parser1,"Opa")   //x = {some: 1}
y = Parser.try_parse(parser1,"Java")  //y = {none}
```

Now let's consider the following parsers:

```
digit1 = parser { case x=[0-9]+: x }
digit2 = parser { case x=([0-9]+): x }
```

Both `digit1` and `digit2` accept a number string like "5", "100", and both will assign the value to the identifier x. If we feed the parser `digit1` with the string "100", x will be the parsing result of the string: a list of characters ['1','0','0']. If we feed the string "100" to parser `digit2`, x will be the input string: 100. So, if we want to get hold of the input string, we need to put the expression in parentheses.

Let's move it a little further; consider the following parser:

```
abs_parser = parser{
   case x=("+"?[0-9]+): Int.of_string("{x}")
   case x=("-"[0-9]+) : 0 - Int.of_string("{x}")
}
x = Parser.try_parse(abs_parser,"-100") // x = {some: 100}
```

This parser accepts an integer string and returns the absolute value. You may figure out how it works with the previous knowledge. Note that even if the expression of PEG looks like a regular expression, they are different.

Summary

This chapter has introduced you to the basic syntax in Opa programming, including datatypes, functions, records, tuples, lists, maps, patterns, and parsers. This is the basic knowledge that we should know to make a good Opa program. With the previous knowledge, we will see how to develop a web application in the next chapter.

Developing Web Applications

3

Opa is designed for rapid and secure web development. In this chapter, we will talk about the fundamental knowledge about developing a web application in Opa.

Starting a web server

The first thing we need for a web application is a web server. In this section we will see how to start a web server using Opa.

A simple example

As a web application, resources such as web pages, images, and audios need to be served to users; therefore, we need an HTTP server. Let's think for a moment about how we would do that in PHP. The typical setup would be an Apache HTTP server with mod_php5 installed.

With Opa, things are a bit different. We not only implement our application, but also the whole HTTP server. In fact, our web application and its web server are basically the same. Our code will be translated into Node.js script after compilation, and will be run with Node.js. The benefit of integrating the server with a web application is increased security. Let's just start with a simple example:

```
Server.start(Server.http, {text: "hello Opa"})
```

Save this code into a file, `301.opa` for example, then compile and run it. The two concluding dashes are needed to launch the web application after it has completed the compilation:

```
$ opa 301.opa --
```

The output will be:

```
Http serving on http://localhost:8080
```

Type this address in your browser and you will see something like this:

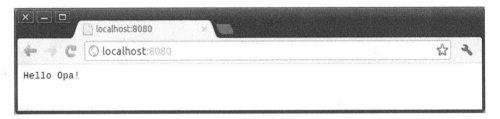

The server module

We have started a web server and run our first Opa web application with the function `Server.start`. Let's now take a detailed look at this function:

```
void start(Server.conf arg1, Server.handler handler)
```

The function starts a web server with two parameters, the first is configuration information and the second is request handler. The `Server.conf` type is the configuration for the server. It is a record type with the following fields:

```
type Server.conf = {
  int port,                        //port server runs on
  ip netmask,                      //netmask
  Server.encryption encryption,//secure config if using https
  String name                      //server name
}
```

In most cases, we do not want to define all the elements in this type. We can extend from the static value `Server.http`. `Server.http` is a predefined default configuration with port equal to 8080 and the server protocol is http, and the default configuration for https is `Server.https`. In the following two lines, we are reusing the `Server.http` configuration, replacing port 8080 by port 8088 by using the instruction `with port: 8088`.

```
conf = {Server.http with port: 8088}
Server.start(conf,{text: "Hello Opa!"})
```

 You can also run your application with the –p option to change the port, which will override this.

Our web server will need to answer differently to different requests, depending on which URL was being requested. Therefore, we will need `Server.handler` to handle these requests. The `Server.handler` type is much more complicated than the `Server.conf` type. It defines how our web server will handle the incoming requests. It's a variant with eight cases:

```
type Server.handler =
  {string text} or
  {string title, (-> xhtml) page} or
  {stringmap(resource) resources} or
  {(Uri.relative -> resource) dispatch} or
  {Server.filter filter, (Uri.relative -> resource) dispatch} or
  {Server.registrable_resource register} or
  {Parser.general_parser(resource) custom} or
  list(Server.handler)
```

In the example at the beginning of this chapter, we used the simplest case — `{string text}`. It accepts all the requests and just shows some text on the page. Let's see how the second case, `{string title, (-> xhtml) page}`, works:

```
Server.start(Server.http, {
  title: "Opa world"
  page : function(){ <h1>Hello Opa!</h1> }
})
```

The second case also handles all the requests, but it servers a single page. The field page is a function with the type `void -> xhtml`, which indicates that the function accepts no parameter and produces a value of the type `xhtml`. We will talk about XHTML later; the result looks like this:

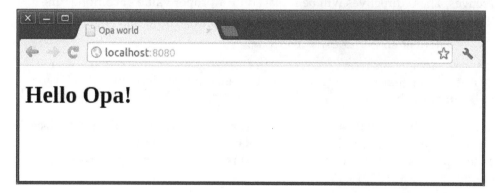

We can notice from this screenshot that, compared to the first example, what has changed is that the web page we sent to the browser includes HTML markup that the web browser renders as a heading type.

Dispatching requests

We have gone through the first two cases of `Server.handler`. They are both simple and accept all requests. But in real web applications, requests and responses are much more complicated, and the web server should respond differently according to different requests. This section we will cover the remaining cases of `Server.handler` and will show how to handle different types of requests.

The resource handler

A resource handler is often used to serve static resources such as images and sounds. The case `{stringmap(resource) resources}` performs on a non-decoded URI (Uniform Resource Identifier), and returns a resource that the URI matches with the resource's stringmap. To make it clear, let's suppose there are three images in the directory `res`: `opa1.png`, `opa2.png`, and `opa3.png`.

If we create the resources stringmap manually, it should look like this:

```
"res/opa1.png" -> a resource of opa1.png
"res/opa2.png" -> a resource of opa2.png
"res/opa3.png" -> a resource of opa3.png
```

The relative URI is the key and the resource of the `.png` file is the value, that is, `"res/opa1.png"` is the key and `opa1.png`, as a resource, is the value. If the user tries to access the URL `http://localhost:8080/res/opa1.png`, the non-decoded relative URI will be `res/opa1.png`. The server will try to find the corresponding resource `opa1.png` and serve it back to the user.

So, how can we add these external files? In Opa, we can use the following two directives. These directives will be replaced by a proper value at compile time:

- `@static_content("foo.png")` is replaced by a function that returns the content of `compile-time foo.png`.

- `@static_resource("foo.png")` is replaced by a value of the resource type `represents foo.png`, with the last modification time, MIME type, among others.

The difference between these two directives is that `@static_content` is replaced by a function, while `@static_resource` is replaced by a resource. Both directives have a counterpart that, instead of processing and returning one file, processes a directory and returns it as a stringmap:

- `@static_content_directory("foo/")` is replaced by a stringmap from file name `f` in the directory `foo/` to `@static_content("f")`

- `@static_resource_directory("foo/")` is replaced by a stringmap from file name `f` in the directory `foo/` to `@static_resource("f")`

Now, it is very clear that if we want to serve resources in the directory res, all we need to do is write the code as follows:

```
Server.start(Server.http,{
  resources: @static_resource_directory("res")
})
```

We can get the resource at http://localhost:8080/res/opa1.png.

The dispatch handler

The resource handler is very useful for static resources. But frequently, the server needs to respond to different requests. The case {(Uri.relative -> resource) dispatch} is just for that. In this case, the request URL is decoded into an Uri.relative record, which is defined as:

```
type Uri.relative ={
  list(string) path,
  list((string, string)) query,
  option(string) fragment,
  bool is_directory,
  bool is_from_root
}
```

Let's suppose the user request URL is http://localhost:8080/admin/ find?name=Li&age=28, the record will be:

```
{ path: [admin,find],          //a list of path
  query: [(name,Li),(age,28)],   //a list of tuple2
  ...}                         //we do not care about the fields here.
```

Having this record, we should return a corresponding resource. Most of the time, pattern matching is used to dispatch requests. Here is an example:

```
function dispatch(uri){
  match(uri){
  case {path:[],...}  : Resource.page("Login",<h1>Login</h1>);
  case {path:["admin"|_],...}:
    Resource.page("Admin", <h1>Admin</h1>);
  case {path:["user",x|_],...}:
    Resource.page("User", <h1>User:{x}</h1>);
  }
}
Server.start(Server.http,{~dispatch})
```

Remember what we discussed about pattern matching in the last chapter? It is not hard to figure out what happens here. Note that pattern matching is not the only way to dispatch requests. You can do almost anything you want to return a resource for a given URI. Besides, we can also add a filter with the case `{Server.filter filter,` `(Uri.relative->resource) dispatch}`:

```
Server.start(Server.http,{
  filter: Server.Filter.path(["opa","packt"]),
  dispatch: function(_){
    Resource.page("opa packt",<h1> Hello Opa!</h1>)
  }
})
```

This code will only allow user to access `http://localhost:8080/opa/packt`.

The register handler

The case `{Server.registrable_resource register}` is an empty request handler, which means it will not handle any request. But it is useful for registering external resources such as `js` and `css`, so that we can use them in our application.

```
Server.start(Server.http,{
  register: [
    {doctype: {html5}},
    {js: ["/res/js/js1.js","/res/js/js2.js"]},
    {css: ["/res/css/style1.css","/res/css/style2.css"]}
  ]
});
```

In this example, we registered the `doctype` as `html5`, and some external JavaScript and CSS. The JavaScript and CSS registered here is application-wide. It means we can use codes from JavaScript and styles from CSS in any page that we create in this application.

The customize handler

The case `{Parser.general_parser(resource) custom}` is the most configurable request handler. The custom parser takes the non-decoded URI from incoming requests as input and computes the corresponding resource. Consider the following example:

```
custom = parser{
  case ("/admin".*) : Resource.page("Admin",<h1>Admin</h1>);
  case ("/user".*) : Resource.page("User",<h1>User</h1>);
  case (.*) : Resource.page("default",<h1>default</h1>);
}
Server.start(Server.http, {~custom});
```

This example will match all requests beginning with `"/admin"` to the admin page created by the code `Resource.page("Admin",<h1>Admin</h1>)`, all requests beginning with `"/user"` to the user page, and all the other requests to a default page. You can refer parser in Opa to get more information about how to deal with more complex cases.

The handlers group

The case list (`Server.handler`) aggregates several request handlers as a group in response to an incoming request. All handlers are tested in the order that they are listed until one succeeds and returns a resource. For example:

```
Server.start(Server.http,[
{resources: @static_resource_directory("resources")},
  {~dispatch},   //we omitted the definition here
  {~custom},     //we omitted the definition here
  {title:"404", page:function(){ <h1>Page Not Found!<h1> }}
]);
```

As a single handler may not be sufficient to deal with all the requests, handlers group is a common solution for most web applications developed by Opa.

Preparing pages

We have discussed how to launch the server and dispatch users' requests. Now it is time for the frontend issue, namely, the web page. Web pages are what users see and interact with. There are numerous technologies that can be used for building excellent web pages, such as PHP, Perl, and Python. But the basic way is using HTML and CSS.

XHTML

In Opa, both HTML and CSS are first class citizens, and are understood and checked by the compiler without you having to wrap them as strings. Having XHTML as a native type implies near-perfect XSS (cross-site scripting) protection. It also means we can easily compose elements, that is, we can write `<div>{foo()}</div>`. HTML values have a predefined `xhtml` type, and there is a built-in syntax for constructing XHTML values. Here is an overview of the syntax for XHTML:

```
// XHTML is a data-type with built-in syntax
xhtml span = <span class="test">Hello Opa!</span>
//named closing tag is optional,
// so are the quotes around literal attributes
another_span = <span class=test>Hello XHTML</>
```

Inserts for both tags and attributes work in XHTML too:

```
function f(class, content){
  <span class="{class}"> {content} </span>
}
```

Creating a page

Usually, we need to serve our web page as a value of the resource type. The function `Resource.page`, or its shortcut `Resource.html`, will help us convert XHTML to a resource. `Resource.page` is defined as:

```
resource page(string title, xhtml body)
```

The first argument is the title of the web page and the second argument is the content written in XHTML. It will return a value of the resource type that we can return to the user. Here is a simple example:

```
function dispatch(_){
  Resource.page("Opa Packt", <h1>Hello Opa!</h1>)
}
Server.start(Server.http,{~dispathc})
```

This code fragment serves all the requests to the web page. `Resource.page` is sufficient for developers in most cases. But if you need more controls, you can refer to `Resource.styled_page` and `Resource.full_page`.

Adding styles

There are many ways to add styles. First, just like XHTML, CSS is a predefined datatype in Opa and we can define CSS in Opa code directly:

```
red_style = css { color: red }
span = <span style={red_style} />
// one can use inserts inside css, i.e. height: {height}px;
function div(width, height, content) {
  <div style={ css { height: {height}px; width: {width}px }}>
    {content}
  </div>
}
```

Another way is using the register handler that we have talked about before:

```
Server.start(Server.http,
  [ {register: {css: ["resources/css/style.css"]}} , ...]
)
```

The stylesheets registered by the register handler are available application-wide, which means that you can use them in any page. If you want to add some page specific stylesheets, the choice will be `Resource.styled_page`. Here is an example:

```
// save this as file: resources/hello.css
.hello1 { font-size: 20pt }
.hello2 { font-size: 12pt }
//save the following code as a file, compile and run it.
function dispatch(_){
  Resource.styled_page("Opa Packt", ["resources/hello.css"],
    <div class="hello1">Hello Opa!</div>
    <div class="hello2">Hello Opa!</div>
  )
}
Server.start(Server.http, [
  {resources: @static_resource_directory("resources")},
  {~dispatch}
])
```

Compile and run this code; the result looks like this:

Handling events

An event handler is a function whose call is triggered by some activity in the user interface. Typical event handlers react to user's clicking (the event is called `click`), pressing enter (event `newline`), moving the mouse (event `mousemove`), or loading the page (event `ready`).

In Opa, an event handler always has the type `Dom.event -> void`. Here is an example:

```
function f1(_){ #test1 = "test1"}
function f2(_){ Dom.set_text(#test2,"clicked"}
function f3(_){ Dom.clear_value(#test3) }
function page(){
  <div id=#test1 onready={f1}></div>
```

```
    <button id=#test2 onclick={f2}>click</button>
    <input id=#test3 onnewline={f3}></input>
    <div id=#test4 onclick={function(_){ jlog("clicked") }}></div>
}
Server.start(Server.http, {title:"Opa Packt", ~page})
```

This code gives an example of how to write event handlers in Opa.

Manipulating DOMs

The Document Object Model (DOM) is a platform and language neutral interface that allows programs and scripts to dynamically access and update the content, structure, and style of documents.

At times, we may want to change the content of a page dynamically. To accomplish this, we will often need to interact with the DOM. Opa provides the module Dom for the purpose of manipulating the contents of the page currently being displayed by the browser. You can use it to add and remove elements to and from the page, to get the contents of a form, or to apply styles or special effects.

DOM selection

The first step that is necessary, in order to use DOMs, is to select the one that you want to work with. Opa provides many ways of selecting elements. You can find all the available selection functions in the module Dom. The most commonly used ones are:

```
Dom.select_id("id")          //select element with a given id
Dom.select_document()        //select the complete document
Dom.select_class("class")    //select elements belongs to a class
Dom.select_children(parent)  //select all children
//and much more, search online Opa API for entry Dom
```

As Dom.select_id is used everywhere and very frequently, Opa provides a shortcut for it. You can simply write #id. For example:

```
#text    //the same as: dom = Dom.select_id("text")
#{test} //insert can be used in this in combination with the
//shortcut notation.
Dom.select_children(#text)
```

Reading values

Often we need to read values or get content from some element of a page. For example, getting user's input or getting the width of an element. Opa provides many get functions to get information of a given Dom item. Consider the following code:

```
<input id=#test type="text" value="test1">test2</input>
x1 = Dom.get_value(#test)                // x1 = test1, x1 is a string
y1 = Dom.get_text(#test)                 // y1 = test2, y1 is a string
x2 = Dom.get_attribute(#test,"type") // x2 = {some: text}
y2 = Dom.get_property(#test,"type")  // y2 = {some: text}
x3 = Dom.get_with(#test)                 //x3 is the width of #test
y3 = Dom.get_height(#test)               //y3 is the height of #test
```

This example illustrates some commonly used functions on Dom, we can find more on online Opa API for the entry Dom. Please do not confuse Dom.get_value with Dom.get_text. The first one will return the content entered by the user (for example, from an input, a menu, and so on), while the second one will return the content inserted in Dom. We can figure that out from the second and third line of the example we just saw.

Updating content

Opa offers three syntactical shortcuts that simplify some of the most common transformations:

```
#identifier = content  //replace the content
#identifier =+ content //prepend the content
#identifier += content //append the content
```

In addition, there are many other functions you can use to add, remove, and update the content of the page:

```
Dom.add_class(#test,"style")      //add a class "style" to #test
Dom.clear_value(#test)              //clear the value of #test
Dom.put_after(#test,#item)        //move #item after #test
Dom.put_before(#test,#item)       //move #item before #test
Dom.put_replace(#test,#item)      //replace #test with #item
Dom.remove(#test)                 //remove dom #test
Dom.remove_class(#test,"style") //remove class "style" in #test
Dom.remove_content(#test)         //remove #test's content
//and for more, search online Opa API for entry Dom
```

Binding an event handler

It is quite common to bind an event handler dynamically at runtime, especially when you are creating controls programmatically. In Opa, we can do this with `Dom.bind`, which is defined as:

```
Dom.event_handler bind(dom dom, Dom.event.kind event,
  ( Dom.event -> void ) handler)
```

The function returns a value of the type `Dom.event_handler`, which you can use to unbind the event handler. Here is an example:

```
<input id=#test type="button" value="bind"></input>
//bind #test's click event with a function
handler = Dom.bind(#test,{click},function(_){ void })
Dom.unbind(#test, handler) //unbind the event handler
```

Animations

Opa provides several techniques for adding animations to a web page. These include simple, standard animations that are frequently used such as fade-in, fade-out, and hide. To apply an animation to a `Dom` item, you should use the function `Dom.transaction`, which is defined as:

```
Dom.transaction transition(dom item, Dom.animation effect)
```

The first parameter is a `Dom` item and the second parameter is the effect you want to apply to this `Dom` item. You can find a full list of effects supported by Opa in the module `Dom.Effect`. Here is an example of animation:

```
function hide(_){
    _ = Dom.transition(#test,Dom.Effect.hide()); void
}
function page(){
  <div id=#test style="width:100px;height:100px;"></div>
  <button id=#btnanim onclick={hide}>Hide</button>
}
Server.start(Server.http,{title:"Opa Packt", ~page})
```

Summary

In this chapter, we first introduced how to start a web server with the function `Server.start`, which is the starting point of our web application. Then we discussed in detail the different cases of `Server.handler`, and how to use them to dispatch user requests. After that, we talked about preparing web pages. Finally, we learned how to change the content of the page dynamically by interacting with DOM.

4
Using Bootstrap

Bootstrap (`http://twitter.github.com/bootstrap`) is a sleek, intuitive, and powerful frontend framework for faster and easier web development. Opa gives you a very easy way to use Bootstrap in your code. In this chapter we will discuss how to use Bootstrap for rapid web development in Opa.

Importing Bootstrap

We have talked about how to import external files (JavaScript, CSS, among others) in the *Resource handler* section of *Chapter 3, Developing Web Applications*. We would have to import all the necessary Bootstrap files if we do that manually. To make it easy, Opa provides some shortcuts for using Bootstrap. Let's get started with an example:

```
import stdlib.themes.bootstrap
function page(){
  <button class="btn btn-primary"
    style="margin:5px">Click</button>
}
Server.start(Server.http,{title:"Opa Packt",~page})
```

All we need is an import statement, and Opa will handle the rest. The result of the above code looks as shown in the following screenshot. We can see that the **Click** button is rendered using the `btn` and the `btn-primary` class, which are provided by Bootstrap.

Actually, we can control the importing in more detail. By doing this, we can prevent loading unnecessary resources and only load what we need. Refer to the following import statements to do this:

```
// import bootstrap css and icons without responsive
import stdlib.themes.bootstrap
// import bootstrap responsive part
import stdlib.themes.bootstrap.responsive
// import bootstrap css (no icons, no responsive)
import stdlib.themes.bootstrap.css
// import bootstrap glyphicons
import stdlib.themes.bootstrap.icons
// import font awesome icons
import stdlib.themes.bootstrap.font-awesome
```

Using classes

Once we have imported Bootstrap CSS, we can use Bootstrap classes and styles. It is just the same as writing code in HTML, that is, `<input class="btn btn-primary"/>`. You can find the complete guide on Bootstrap's website (http://twitter.github.com/bootstrap/base-css.html).

Let's take button for example:

```
import stdlib.themes.bootstrap
function page(){
  <div style="margin:5px">
    <button class="btn btn-large">Large Button</button>
    <button class="btn">Default Button</button>
    <button class="btn btn-primary">Primary Button</button>
    <button class="btn btn-small">Small Button</button>
    <button class="btn btn-mini">Mini Button</button>
  </div>
}
Server.start(Server.http,{title:"Opa Packt",~page})
```

And that's it; it is quite simple to use Bootstrap's classes in Opa, the result looks as follows:

Using icons

Bootstrap includes a set of icons provided by Glyphicons (http://glyphicons.
com/). It has icons that are available in both dark gray and white. Besides, Opa also
includes Font Awesome (http://fortawesome.github.com/Font-Awesome/) icons.

Bootstrap icons

It's very easy to use icons. All icons require <i> with a unique class prefixed with
icon-. To use them, place the following code just about anywhere:

```
<i class="icon-search"></i>
```

The default color is dark gray. If you need to use a white icon, add icon-white
to class. Consider the following example:

```
import stdlib.themes.bootstrap
function page(){
  <div style="margin:5px">
    <button class="btn">
      <i class="icon-search"></i> Search
    </button>
    <button class="btn btn-inverse">
      <i class="icon-search icon-white"></i> Search
    </button>
    <div class="btn-group">
      <a class="btn"><i class="icon-align-left"></i></a>
      <a class="btn"><i class="icon-align-center"></i></a>
      <a class="btn"><i class="icon-align-right"></i></a>
      <a class="btn"><i class="icon-align-justify"></i></a>
    </div>
  </div>
}
Server.start(Server.http,{title:"Opa Packt",~page})
```

The result looks like the following screenshot. We made buttons and a button group
using Bootstrap icons.

Font Awesome icons

Font Awesome is the iconic font designed for use with Twitter Bootstrap. It's designed to be fully backwards compatible with Bootstrap 2.0. The icons in Font Awesome are scalable vector graphics, which means they look awesome at any size. Moreover, you can control icon color, size, shadow, and anything that's possible with CSS. Opa provides the support for Font Awesome in language, so it's very easy for Opa developers to use Font Awesome. Here is an example:

```
import stdlib.themes.bootstrap.css
import stdlib.themes.bootstrap.font-awesome
function page(){
  <div style="margin:5px">
    <button class="btn">
      <i class="icon-search"></i> Search
    </button>
    <button class="btn btn-inverse">
      <i class="icon-search"></i> Search
    </button>
    <button class="btn btn-large">
      <i class="icon-search"></i> Search
    </button>
  </div>
  <div style="margin:5px;font-size:24px">
    <i class="icon-search"></i> Search
  </div>
}
Server.start(Server.http,{title:"Opa Packt",~page})
```

As we can see from the following screenshot, the **Search** icon scales automatically according to the font size:

Using widgets

There are some components that are commonly used in web application, such as alert information, drop-down buttons, button groups, and modal dialogs. Bootstrap has a great support for that, and you can create those widgets in Opa. Let's first take a look at how we create a drop-down button in Opa:

```
import stdlib.themes.bootstrap.css
function page(){
  <div class="btn-group" style="margin:10px">
    <a class="btn dropdown-toggle" data-toggle="dropdown"
      href="#">
      Action <span class="caret"></span>
    </a>
    <ul class="dropdown-menu">
      <li><a href="#">action1</a></li>
      <li><a href="#">action2</a></li>
      <li><a href="#">action3</a></li>
    </ul>
  </div>
}
Server.start(Server.http, [
  {resources: @static_resource_directory("resources")},
  {register: [{js: ["resources/bootstrap.min.js"]}] },
  {title:"Opa Packt", ~page}
])
```

Note that we use `bootstrap.min.js` as an external JavaScript to enable the effect provided by Bootstrap. You can download this file from the Bootstrap website.

The **Action** drop-down button looks as shown in the following screenshot:

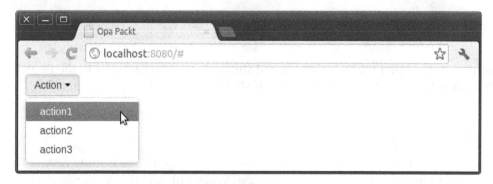

Let's take a look at another example—the modal dialog. Here, we have only shown a code fragment of `function page()`. We omitted the rest of the code because it is identical to the drop-down button code:

```
function page(){
  <div class="modal hide" id=#mymodal>
    <div class="modal-header">
      <button class="close" data-dismiss="modal">x</button>
      <h3>Modal header</h3>
    </div>
    <div class="modal-body"> <p>One fine Body...</p> </div>
    <div class="modal-footer">
      <a href="#" data-dismiss="modal" class="btn">Cancel</a>
    </div>
  </div>
  <a class="btn" data-toggle="modal" href="#mymodal">Show</a>
}
```

Compile and run the code; the result looks like this:

There are some other widgets that are not shown here. You can refer to the Bootstrap home page (`http://twitter.github.com/bootstrap`) for more information.

Summary

As we can see from this chapter, working with Bootstrap in Opa is quite easy. You only need to import the proper resources that you want, and the rest is almost the same as developing in pure HTML. Bootstrap's home page (`http://twitter.github.com/bootstrap`) is a good place to get more information.

5
Communicating between Client and Server

An important difference between Opa and most other web development languages is that other technologies typically require the use of multiple languages in order to write client-side and server-side code, whereas in Opa we can do both using a single language. This gives us the ability to invoke a remote procedure just like a local function. We do not need to send Ajax requests and parse response data ourselves. In this chapter, we will first talk about how to slice server and client code using Opa and what we can do to help the slicer when automatic slicing is not enough. Then, we will introduce three primitives for communication between clients and the server: session, cell, and network.

Client and server slicing

Opa allows developers to write the server and client code both in the same language within the same module. And even better, the Opa slicer automates the calls between the client and the server. No more manually written Ajax calls or value serialization is needed!

A simple example

Let's get started with a simple example. Suppose we want to send our name to the server and request the server to respond with the words "Say hello to [name] from server":

This is quite simple and can be accomplished with almost any language that we are familiar with. Typically, you would send an Ajax request to the server with name as request data, and the server will respond with a JSON object containing the string we want. The following code fragment demonstrates how we can do this using jQuery for the client-side code and ASP as server-side code:

```
//code fragment on server side: ajax.aspx
Response.ContentType = "application/json";
Response.Write("{result: 'Say hello to "
+ Request["Name"] + "from server.'}");

//request code fragment on client side
$.post( "ajax.aspx",              //request url
{Name:"Li"},                      //request data
function (data, textStatus){},    //call back
"json");                          //data type
```

With Opa, things become even easier. We can skip the step of sending an Ajax request, and we also don't need to parse the JSON response data ourselves. We only need to write a normal function with a server tag and invoke the function from the client. Here is the complete code:

```
server function sayhello(name){
  "Say hello to " + name + " from server."
}
function page(){
  <input id=#name type="text"/>
  <input type="button" value="hello" onclick={function(_){
```

```
    #text = sayhello(Dom.get_value(#name))
  }}/>
  <h3 id=#text></h3>
}
Server.start(Server.http,{title:"Opa Packt",~page})
```

In the preceding code, we add a `server` tag before the `sayhello` function to indicate that it is a function on the server side, and we invoke this function on the client as a normal client-side function. If the `server` tag is removed, the `sayhello` function will be a client-side function in this example, and there will be no communication between the client and the server.

Slicing annotations

The `server` tag tells the Opa complier to put the `sayhello` function on the server side. Opa is a language that can be executed both on a client and a server, but at some point during the compilation process, it must be decided on which side does the code actually end up, and whether there are any remote calls.

If the developer does not provide the slicing information by adding the slicing annotations (server, client, and both) before a function or a module, then Opa will perform the slicing job automatically. The rules for slicing that Opa follows by default are quite simple. Opa will implement the function on both the server as well as the client if possible. If it is not possible to implement the function both on the server and the client, then Opa will implement the function either on the server or on the client, depending on where it is possible to implement the function. For instance, if we remove the `server` tag from the `sayhello` function in the previous example, then Opa's slicer will implement the function twice, once on the server and once on the client. As a result, the invocation is no longer a remote call but a local call.

When automatic slicing is not enough, for example, if we want a function to only be available on the server side or client side, we can add slicing annotations before the function keyword to tell the slicer where a declaration should end up. There are three slicing annotations: **server**, **client** and **both**.

- **server**: Opa will implement the function on the server (but it does not mean that it will not be visible for the code running on the client)
- **client**: Opa will implement the code on the client (but it does not mean that it will not be visible for the code running on the server)
- **both**: The function is implemented both on the server as well as the client

It is easy to understand what the **server** and **client** mean, but the **both** keyword is less intuitive. The problem is that a definition can have arbitrary side effects.

 Side effect: In computer science, a function or expression is said to have a side effect if, in addition to returning a value, it also modifies some state or has an observable interaction with calling functions or the outside world.

Therefore, there are two possible meanings: either the side effect is executed on both sides or the side effect is executed once on the server and the resulting value is shared between the two sides. By default, the slicer duplicates some side effects such as printing and avoids duplicating the allocation of mutable structures.

Consider the following example:

```
println("Hello Opa!")
counter = Mutable.make(0)
function page(){ <h1>...</h1> }
Server.start(Server.http,{title:"Opa Packt", ~page})
```

If we compile and run the preceding code, it will print "Hello Opa!" on the server and the client both, but will create only one unique mutable variable called `counter` that is shared between the client and the server.

But, we sometimes do want to duplicate the declaration on both sides. In that case, we can use the `@both_implem` directive. For example:

```
@both_implem counter = Mutable.make(100)
```

This will create a mutable variable `counter` at the startup of the server and in each client.

Module slicing

When a slicing annotation refers to a module, it becomes the default slicing annotation for its components, but can be overridden by annotating the component with another annotation. Consider the following example:

```
server module Logic{
  function f1() { println("function 1") }
  client function f2(){ println("function 2") }
}
function page(){
  <div onready={function(_){ Logic.f1(); Logic.f2() }}></div>
}
Server.start(Server.http,{title:"Opa Packt", ~page})
```

Because we put `server` before the `Logic` module, function `f1` will end up on the server side. But we override the slicing annotation of function `f2` with `client`, so function `f2` will be on the client side. We invoke both `f1` and `f2` when the page is ready, `f1` will print **function1** on the server side while `f2` will print **function2** on the client side. The following screenshot shows the result as expected:

Expression slicing

Sometimes, we want to have a different behavior on the server and on the client. We can use the `@sliced_expr` directive to do this. Consider the following example:

```
side = @sliced_expr({server: "server", client:"client"})
println(side) //will print "server" on server side and "client"
            // on client side.
function page(){ <h1>Test Page</h1> }
Server.start(Server.http, {title:"Opa Packt", ~page});
```

The preceding code will print "server" on the server side and "client" on the client side.

Client and server communication

Opa provides three primitives for communicating between clients and the server: session, cell, and network. We can use these three primitives to exchange messages between clients and servers.

Session

A session is a one-way asynchronous communication between the client and the server. A session can be created on a server or on a client, and can be shared between several servers.

To create a session, use either `Session.make` or `Session.NonBlocking.make`. The `Session.make` function creates a session that handles all messages in the background, but only one message at a time. This ensures absolute consistency on the state of the session, but may not be appropriate for all applications.

In contrast, the `Session.NonBlocking.make` function creates a session that can handle any number of messages simultaneously. This ensures maximal responsiveness, but the message handler cannot be certain that it is holding the latest value of the state. Let's have a look at how `Session.make` is declared:

```
channel(`message) make(`state state,
(`state, `message -> Session.instruction(`state) on_message)
```

The first parameter `state` is the initial state of the session. The second parameter is a message handler for this session. The message handler will be invoked when messages are sent to this session. The return value of this function is a channel, which we can use to send messages to the session by using the `Session.send` function.

Consider the following example: suppose we want to send a string to the server through a session such that if the state of this session is an odd number, then whatever we send to the server is printed in uppercase. In contrast, if the state of this session is even then we print in lowercase. The code is as follows:

```
channel(string) s = Session.make(0,function(state,msg){
  if(mod(state,2) == 0) println(String.to_upper(msg))
  else                   println(String.to_lower(msg))
  {set:state+1}          //update the state of this session
})
function page(){
  <input type="text" id=#text/>
  <input type="button" value="send" onclick={function(_){
        Session.send(s, Dom.get_value(#text))
  }}/>
}
Server.start(Server.http, {title:"Opa Packt", ~page})
```

If we compile and run the preceding code, then we will see the following result on the server:

```
winbomb@ubuntu: ~/workspace/opapackt/ch05
winbomb@ubuntu:~/workspace/opapackt/ch05$ opa 508.opa --
Http serving on http://ubuntu:8080
KFDJASFDJADFA
dadadfdasf
FKLDAJF;DLKAJ
dfafdaf
DASFSFASFAS
dfafdada
```

Cell

A cell is a session in which sending messages produces return values. It's a two-way synchronous communication between the client and the server. We can create a cell with Cell.make and call it with Cell.call. In the following example, the cell does almost the same thing as we had described in the previous example, but it returns the string to the client instead of printing it on the server. Here is the code fragment:

```
s = Cell.make(0,function(state,msg){
    text =  if(mod(state,2) == 0)    String.to_upper(msg)
            else                     String.to_lower(msg)
    {return: text, instruction: {set: state+1}}
});
function page(){
    <input type="text" id=#text/>
    <input type="button" value="send" onclick={function(_){
        #result = Cell.call(s, Dom.get_value(#text))
    }}/>
    <h2 id=#result></h2>
}
Server.start(Server.http, {title:"Opa Packt", ~page})
```

Network

A network is an infrastructure for broadcasting information to observers. Observers may be sessions or functions located on the same machine or on any client or server.

We can create a network with the Network.empty() function or construct a network that is automatically shared between servers with the Network.cloud(key) function.

We can observe a network with the `Network.observe(cb,network)` function, where `cb` is a callback function that is executed when a message is received on the network. To send a message to all observers of a network, use `Network.broadcast(msg,network)`.

The following example is a very simple chat application; the client will observe the network when its page is ready, and it will broadcast a message when the send button is triggered. We will learn to build a more sophisticated web chat application in *Chapter 9, Building a Chat Application*.

```
Network.network(string) n = Network.empty();
function ready(_){
    _ = Network.observe(function(msg){ println("{msg}") },n)
    void
}
function page(){
    <div onready={ready}>
        <input type="text" id=#text/>
        <input type="button" value="send" onclick={function(_){
            Network.broadcast(Dom.get_value(#text),n)
        }}/>
    </div>
}
Server.start(Server.http,{title:"Opa Packt", ~page})
```

Compile and run the preceding code, then open the web application in several browsers. We can communicate between browsers by sending the messages that we input. Here is a screenshot:

Summary

In this chapter, we first talked about the Opa slicer. If we do not provide slicing information, the slicer will try to put the code on both sides whenever it is possible and will put the code on only one side when there is no way to put the code on both sides. When this automatic slicing is not enough, we can add slicing annotations (server, client, and both) before functions and modules to tell the slicer on which side we want our code to end. Then, we talked about the three primitives for communicating between clients and servers. Session is a one-way asynchronous communication, cell is a two-way synchronous communication, and network is for broadcasting messages to any number of observers.

6
Binding with Other Languages

As mentioned in the *Register handler* section of *Chapter 3, Developing Web Applications*, we can register external JavaScript code by utilizing the `Resource.register_external_js` function. But, this is not how we call external JavaScript functions from Opa. This is only true when we wish to invoke Node.js functions. In such cases, we instead bind external functions with Opa's binding ability. In this chapter, we will explain how to bind external JavaScript or Node.js functions.

Binding JavaScript

Opa allows binding of the external functions through its **Binding System Library (BSL)**. If we surf the source code of Opa, we will find in many places that Opa binds JavaScript in its source code. Actually, Opa provides three forms of binding syntax: `classic`, `jsdoc`, and `new`. The jsdoc syntax is now (Opa 1.1.0) the default.

The first example

Let's get started with a binding example of JavaScript. Suppose we have finished a `test` function in the `test.js` JavaScript file, and then we want to use it in the `601.opa` Opa file.

The content of the `test.js` file is as follows:

```
/**
 * A test function of Opa binding
 * @register {string -> void}
 */
function test(str){
        alert(str);
}
```

We registered the `test` function using the annotation `@register {string -> void}`. This indicates that the function being registered has the `string -> void` type. To invoke the `test` function in Opa code, we designate the function as an external JavaScript function by surrounding the name of the function with the special designator `%%`. In the following example, we call the JavaScript `test` function located in `test.js` from within the `601.opa` file:

```
function page(){
    <input type="button" value="click" onclick={function(_){
        %%test.test%%("Hello Opa!")
    }}/>
}
Server.start(Server.http,{title:"Opa Packt", ~page})
```

We call the function using `%%test.test%%("Hello Opa!")`. The word "test" appears in this example twice, once preceding the dot and once after the dot. The first "test" is the name of the plugin module; in this case it is the filename of `test.js`. The second "test" is the name of the function that we define in this file. We can compile the JavaScript code and Opa code together by using the following command line:

opa test.js 601.opa   --

By default, the registered function name is identical to the original function name that we defined in the JavaScript file. However, we can modify the name as follows:

```
/**
 * @register {string -> void} test2
 */
function test(str){
        alert(str);
}
```

Note that we added `test2` to the end of the line that we used to register the function. Now, we can invoke it using `%%test.test2%%("Hello Opa!")`.

---

[52]

Using external types

Sometimes, we may want to handle the Opa types such as list (`a), option ('a), or Opa external types that we defined in Opa in JavaScript. In the following example, we define a type Student and its variable stu; variable lst is the Opa type list(string), which we may not use in JavaScript directly; and the variable arr is an external type.

```
/** 602.opa */
type Student = {string name, bool sex, int age} //Type we defined
Student      stu = {name:"Li", sex: {true}, age: 28}
list(string) lst = ["I ","Like ","Opa ","!"];   //Opa's types
llarray(int) arr = @llarray(1,2,3,4);           //Extern types
function page(){
    <input type="button" value="func1()" onclick={function(_){
        %%test2.func1%%(stu)
    }}/>
    <input type="button" value="func2()" onclick={function(_){
        %%test2.func2%%(lst)
    }}/>
    <input type="button" value="func3()" onclick={function(_){
        %%test2.func3%%(arr)
    }}/>
}
Server.start(Server.http, {title:"Opa Packt", ~page});
```

In our JavaScript file, we define three functions: func1, func2, and func3. func1 accepts type Student, func2 accepts type list(string), and func3 accepts type llarray(int). All these three functions do nothing but print the content of their respective arguments to the console. The first thing we should do is declare Opa types and external types with the directives @opaType and @externType respectively.

The content of the file test2.js is as follows:

```
/** test2.js */
/** @opaType list('a) */
/** @opaType Student */
/** @externType llarray('a) */
/** @register {opa[Student] -> void} */
function func1(stu){
    console.log("func1: "+ stu.name +" , "+stu.sex+", "+stu.age);
}
/** @register {opa[list(string)] -> void} */
function func2(lst){
```

```
    //use list2js to convert Opa list to js list.
    var lst2 = list2js(lst);
    for(var i=0; i<lst2.length; i++)
        console.log("func2: " + lst2[i]);
}
/** @register {llarray(int) -> void} */
function func3(arr){
    for(var i=0; i<arr.length; i++)
        console.log("func3: " + arr[i]);
}
```

Compile and run `opa test2.js 602.opa --`

Press *F12* in your Chrome browser to open the developer tool and you will see the output we printed in the console.

Binding Node.js

Binding Node.js code is just as easy as binding JavaScript. Let's see an example: suppose we have written a function called `calcMD5` in a Node.js file called `test.nodejs`. The function accepts a string and returns its MD5 hash value. The `test.nodejs` file contains the following code:

```
/** test.nodejs */
var crypto = require('crypto');
```

```
/**
 * Calculates the MD5 hash value of a string.
 * @register {string -> string}
 */
var calcMD5 = function(str){
    return crypto.createHash('md5').update(str).digest('hex');
}
```

As we can see from the preceding code, we bind Node.js in the same manner that we previously used to bind the client-side JavaScript code. We also invoke it in the same way:

```
/** 603.opa */
md5 = %%test.calcMD5%%("Hello Opa!");
println("MD5 value: {md5}");
```

And finally, we compile and run the application:

```
opa test.nodejs 603.opa --
```

The result is as shown in the following screenshot:

```
winbomb@ubuntu: ~/workspace/opapackt/ch06
winbomb@ubuntu:~/workspace/opapackt/ch06$ opa test.nodejs 603.opa --js-bypa
ss-syntax jsdoc --
MD5 value: 3e11f0d269794a88ff70a050c1811dd5
winbomb@ubuntu:~/workspace/opapackt/ch06$
```

Binding external functions using the classic syntax

We can also bind external functions with the `classic` syntax. The `classic` syntax is a little different from the `jsdoc` syntax. It uses `##` to register functions. A typical registration body is as follows:

```
##register function_name: function_type
##args(argment_list)
{
    //function body
}
```

In `classic` syntax, `test2.js` will contain the following code:

```
##opa-type Student
##opa-type list('a)
##extern-type llarray('a)
##register func1: opa[Student] -> void
##args(stu)
{
  console.log("func1: "+ stu.name +" , "+stu.sex+", "+stu.age);
}


##register func2: opa[list(string)] -> void
##args(lst)
{
    var lst2 = list2js(lst);
    for(var i=0; i<lst2.length; i++)
        console.log("func2: " + lst2[i]);
}


##register func3: llarray(int) -> void
##args(arr)
{
  for(var i=0; i<arr.length; i++)
        console.log("func3: " + arr[i]);
}
```

We can now compile the rewritten file using the following command:

```
opa test2.js 601.opa --js-bypass-syntax classic
```

Summary

In this chapter, we talked about how to bind client-side JavaScript and server-side Node.js into our Opa code. We described two syntax variations: `classic` syntax and `jsdoc` syntax. The examples used in this chapter demonstrated that binding JavaScript and Node.js is quite trivial in Opa.

7
Working with Databases

Database queries are also written directly with Opa. Opa currently (Opa 1.1.1) supports the NoSQL databases MongoDB and CouchDB as well as the SQL database Postgres. Postgres is still a work in progress and more databases are planned for future releases. Opa provides many unique advanced operators and automates the database queries for maximal productivity. In this chapter, we will talk briefly about how to work with MongoDB.

A quick start to MongoDB

First, we need to download (http://www.mongodb.org/downloads), install, and run (http://docs.mongodb.org/manual/installation/) the MongoDB server. After MongoDB has been installed properly, let's get started with a simple example:

```
database int /counter = 0;
function page(){
    <h1 id="text">Hello {/counter}</h1>
    <input type="button" value="click" onclick={function(_){
        /counter++
        #text = "Hello {/counter}"
    }}/>}
Server.start(Server.http, {title:"Opa Packt", ~page})
```

In the first line of the preceding code, we define a /counter database path that holds an integer. A database path describes a position in the database, and we can read, write, update, and delete the data through a database path. Note that the data type of the path cannot be omitted.

The preceding database is unnamed; we can give a name to the database, for example:

```
database testdb {
    int /counter = 0;
}
```

In this way, we should read data from the path `/testdb/counter`. Now, let's compile and run the code:

```
$ opa 701.opa --
```

When the application starts, it will try to launch the MongoDB server if the server is not already running, and it will store data on the default location `~/.opa/mongo/data`. If the server is already running, the application will try to connect to the server. However, we can also use the options `--db-local` and `--db-remote` to let the program connect to specific databases as we want:

- `--db-local:dbname [/path/to/db]`: This uses a local database stored at the specified location in the file-system
- `--db-remote:dbname [username:password@]hostname[:port]`: This uses a remote database accessible at a given remote location

For example:

```
$ ./701.js --db-local:testdb
$ ./701.js --db-local:testdb ~/data/mongo
$ ./701.js --db-remote:testdb localhost:27017
$ ./701.js --db-remote:testdb admin:admin@localhost:27017
```

Database manipulation

We can manipulate data through database paths. The following piece of code declares a `testdb` database and defines several paths:

```
type Student = {int id, string name, int age}
database testdb {
    int                /basic/i        //Basic type int
    float              /basic/f        //Basic type float
    string             /basic/s        //Basic type string
    Student            /stu            //Record
    list(string)       /lst            //List
    intmap(Student)    /stumap         //Map
    Student            /stuset[{id}]       //Set
}
```

Type student that we defined ourselves. In addition to this type, our example covers the datatypes that are most frequently used in databases.

Each database path has a default value. Whenever we attempt to read a value that does not exist (either because it was never initialized or it has been removed), the default value is returned. The following list shows the default values for different types:

- The default value for an integer (int) is 0
- The default value for a floating-point number (float) is 0.0
- The default value for a string is ""
- The default value for a record is the record of default values
- The default value for a sum type is the value that best resembles the empty case (for example, {none} for option, {nil} for list, and so on)

We can define an application-specific default value by assigning a value when we declare a path, for example:

```
database testdb {
    int      /basic/i = 10
    string   /basic/s = "default"
    Student  /stu = {id: 0, name: "unknown", age: 25}
}
```

To read data from the database, just use a database path, for example:

```
int i = /testdb/basic/i
Student stu = /testdb/stu
```

We can prefix the path with a question mark (?) then give the path a value that is one of two options, whereby {some: x} indicates that the value of that path is x, and {none} indicates that the path has not been written to yet, for instance:

```
match (?/testdb/basic/i) {
case {none}: println("unknown");
case {some: x}: println("{x}");
}
```

The preceding example prints **unknown** if the path /testdb/basic/i has not been written to yet or has been removed, otherwise it prints the value of the path.

To write or update the database path, use a operator =. We can also use <- to assign the value, it's the same as =. For example:

```
/testdb/basic/i = 10
/testdb/basic/i <- 10 //the same as above
/testdb/basic/s = "my new string"
/testdb/stu = {id: 1, name: "Li", age: 28}In addition, you can also
use the following shortcuts to update integers in database:
/testdb/basic/i++;      //add the integer i by 1
/testdb/basic/i += 5;   //add the integer i by 5
/testdb/basic/i -= 10;  //minus the integer i by 10
```

To delete data held at a path, use the Db.remove(@path) function, where @path is a reference to a path. We can get a path reference by adding an @ sign before the path, for example:

```
Db.remove(@/testdb/basic/i)
Db.remove(@/testdb/stu)
```

Records

With records, we can do complete reads and updates in the same manner as for basic types:

```
stu = /testdb/stu;                                 //read record
/testdb/stu = {id: 1, name: "Li", age: 28} //update record
```

Sometimes, we need to enforce that the record should be modified only as a whole. This is known as **full modification**. If a record is declared as being subject to full modification, we must update all fields at once when performing modifications. We add the full keyword after a database path in order to indicate that this path is subject to full modification. If a given path has not been declared for full modification, we can cross record boundaries and access or update only chosen fields by including them in the path. Consider the following example:

```
type Student = {int id, string name, int age}
database testdb {
    Student /stu1
    Student /stu2
    /stu2 full          //declare /stu2 as full modification
}
/testdb/stu1/name = "Li" //OK
/testdb/stu2 = {id:1, name: "Li", age: 28} //OK
/testdb/stu2/name = "Li" //error: will not compile
```

We declared /stu2 for full modification by adding the /stu2 full statement. Therefore, the compiler reported an error for the last line (/testdb/stu2/name = "Li") of the preceding code, in which we tried modifying a single field of the record, namely the name field.

Lists

As mentioned in the *Lists* section of *Chapter 2, Basic Syntax*, lists in Opa are just recursive records. We can manipulate lists in the same manner as records. However, as the datatype list is used frequently, Opa provides shortcuts that are specific to lists:

```
/testdb/lst = ["I", "Love", "Opa", "!"] //Update an entire list
/testdb/lst pop              // Removes first element of a list
/testdb/lst shift            // Removes last element of a list
/testdb/lst <+ "element"     // Append an element
/testdb/lst <++ ["How", "about", "you"] // Append several elements
/testdb/lst <--* "element"              // Remove an element
/testdb/lst <-- ["How", "about", "you"] // Remove several elements
```

Sets and maps

We can update sets and maps in the same way as lists, however, the way we access the elements is different. We can fetch a single value from a given set or map by referencing it by its primary key, for example:

```
stu = /testdb/stuimap[1] //find element whose key is 1
stu = /testdb/stuset[1]   //find element whose primary key is 1
stu = /testdb/stuset[{id:1}] //the same as above
/testdb/stuset[{id:1}] = {name: "Li"}  //update the chosen item
```

Furthermore, we can query a set of values by adding the query condition inside the square bracket, for example:

```
/testdb/stuset[id < 10] <- {age: 25}
/testdb/stuset[age >= 25] <- {age++}
```

We will look at queries in more detail in the following section.

Querying data

As we mentioned in the previous section, database sets and maps are two types of collections that allows the organization of multiple instances of data in the database. We can query a set of values using the following operators:

```
== expr: equals expr
!= expr: not equals expr
< expr:  lesser than expr
<= expr: lesser than or equals expr
> expr:  greater than expr
>= expr: greater than or equals expr
in expr: "belongs to" expr, where expr is a list
q1 or q2: satisfy query q1 or q2
q1 and q2: satisfy both queries, q1 and q2
not q: does not satisfy q
{f1 q1, f2 q2, ...}: the database field f1 satisfies q1, field f2
satisfies q2 etc.
```

Furthermore, we can specify some querying options as follows:

- `skip n`: Here `expr` should be an expression of type `int` and it skip the first *n* results.

- `limit n`: Here `expr` should be an expression of type `int`, returns a maximum of *n* results.

- `order fld (, fld)+`: Here `fld` specifies an order. `fld` can be a single identifier or a list of identifiers specifying the fields on which the ordering should be based. Identifiers can optionally be prefixed with + or - to specify the ascending or descending order. Finally, it is possible to choose the order dynamically with `<ident>=<expr>`, where `<expr>` should be of type `{up}` or `{down}`.

The following piece of code gets the next 50 results for students whose age is above 20 and below 45, and they will be ordered by age (ascending) first and then ordered by `id` (descending):

```
dbset(Student, _) stus = /testdb/stuset[age >= 20 and age <= 45; skip
50; limit 50; order +age, -id]
```

We can create even more complicated query conditions by combining query expressions together. The query operation returns a `dbset`. A `dbset` is a collection that holds the query result. Therefore, we can iterate over the `dbset`. Consider the following code fragment. It queries all students whose name is `Li` and prints them out:

```
dbset(Student,_) lis = /testdb/stuset[name == "Li"]
iter it = DbSet.iterator(lis)
Iter.iter(function(li){
println("{li}")
},it)
```

Summary

In this chapter, we toured the basic techniques of working with databases. We first gave a very simple example. Then, we discussed how to manipulate data, including retrieving data from databases, writing or updating data, and removing data. We covered both basic types and complex types such as record, list, map, and set. Finally, we talked about how to query data from sets and maps.

8
Internationalization

In this chapter, we will talk about **internationalization (i18n)**. It is abbreviated as i18n because there are 18 letters between the initial *i* and the final *n*. Opa now provides two approaches for i18n: the internal approach and the external approach. To utilize the internal approach, we include translation functions directly inside our Opa code. If, however, we wish to separate the translation from our main code, then we can do so by using the external approach. To make it clear, we will discuss a very simple application that displays the word "hello" in three different languages: English, French, and Chinese.

Internal approach

Opa now provides support for translation by means of the `@i18n` directive. We can put a translation function inside the `@i18n` directive, and it will be replaced by a proper value according to different languages. An example is worth a thousand words, so let's get started with a simple example:

```
import stdlib.web.client
hello = function {
  case "en": "Hello"
  case "fr": "Bonjour"
  case "zh": "你好"
  default: "Hi"
}
function page(){
  <h1> {@i18n(hello)} </h1>
  <input type="button" value="English" onclick={set_lang("en")}/>
  <input type="button" value="French"  onclick={set_lang("fr")}/>
  <input type="button" value="Chinese" onclick={set_lang("zh")}/>
}
function set_lang(lang)(_){
```

```
    I18n.set_lang(lang)
    Client.reload()
}
Server.start(Server.http, {title:"Opa Packt", ~page})
```

Save this code into a file, `801.opa`, then compile and run it with the following command:

opa 801.opa --

The result looks as shown in the following screenshot:

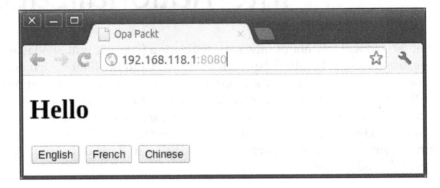

The page shows **Hello** in three different languages: English, French, and Chinese, and we can change the language by clicking on the language buttons.

As we can see from the code, we internationalize the page by enclosing a translation function, `hello`, in the `@i18n` directive—`@i18n(hello)`.

The function `hello` maps from the language code (for example, "en", "fr", and "zh", of the type `I18n.language`) to a string. Note that the function `hello` is written in a convenient way, in that .... This notation is permitted if the initial lines of code in a function consist of matching its parameter against some values, as we do in the `hello` function. The corresponding long notation would be:

```
hello = function(lang){
  match(lang){
    case "en": "Hello"
      ...
  }
}
```

Also note that the return type of a translation function is not restricted to the type String; an XHTML fragment can also be returned from the function:

```
hello = function{
  case "en": <font color="red"> Hello </font>
  case "fr": <font color="blue"> Bonjour </font>
  case "zh": <font color="green"> 你好 </font>
  default:   <font color="yellow"> Hi </font>
}
```

Now that we have reviewed how to write a translation function, we now need to clarify how users control the language of the website they are seeing. The module I18n, the internationalization module, contains the answer. The I18n.lang() function returns the currently selected language. Note that this is not the language of the browser, it is the language that the user selected. We can change the selected language programmatically by invoking the function I18n.set_lang(lang). This is just what we did after clicking on the three language buttons **English, French**, and **Chinese** in the example we just saw. This function allows us to change the language for a specific client. The language our program defines is then stored in a cookie. Since the changes our program makes will only take effect during the next page request, to make them effective right away our program must refresh the page by calling the function Client.reload.

External approach

The internal approach suffers from one important problem, that is, it mixes the source code and the translations. The remedy for this problem is the external approach. Using it, we can separate the program code and the translations.

To use external translations, we use the same @i18n directive, but we provide it with a key string instead of a function. Thus, @i18n(hello) can be replaced by:

```
@i18n("hello")
```

Here is an example of an external approach:

```
//802.opa
function page(){
  <div onready={function(_) { I18n.set_lang("fr") }}>
    <h1>{@i18n("hello")}</h1>
  </div>
}
Server.start(Server.http, {title:"Opa Packt", ~page})
```

Save the file as `802.opa`. If we do not provide any translation, `@i18n("hello")` will be replaced by the string `"hello"`. How do we add the translation? The solution is to compile our source code with the translation switch `--i18n-template-opa`:

```
opa 802.opa --i18n-template-opa --i18n-pkg trans --i18n-dir langs
```

Make a directory named `langs` and execute this line. This will create a file named `trans.opa` in the `langs` directory. The option `--i18n-pkg` specifies the package name of the translation code. If it is not provided, the default name will be `linking.translation`. The option `--i18n-dir` specifies the directory of translation code. If it is not provided, the current directory will be used. The content of `trans.opa` looks as follows:

```
package trans
import stdlib.core.i18n

// Template for 801.opa
// "hello"
// string, 15
__i18n_5d41402abc4b2a76b9719d911017c592()= match I18n.lang()
    _   -> "hello"
```

The file contains all the messages that require translation in all the source code files of a given package. The long sequence `5d41402abc4b2a76b9719d911017c592` is an automatically generated identifier.

Next, we must edit the translation file that Opa generated, adding our translation messages to the file. In our example case, for instance, we could add the following translation instructions:

```
package trans
import stdlib.core.i18n
// Template for 801.opa
// "hello"
// string, 15
__i18n_5d41402abc4b2a76b9719d911017c592()= match I18n.lang()
  "en" -> "Hello"
  "fr" -> "Bonjour"
  "zh" -> "你好"
    _   -> "hello"
```

The translation file is a normal Opa file, and its contents can be intuitively comprehended. Such a notation is called classic syntax. We must tell the compiler that we are utilizing classic Opa source code when we compile the translation:

```
opa --parser classic langs/trans.opa
```

And finally, compile our source code with the translation:

```
opa 801.opa --i18n-dir langs --i18n-pkg trans
```

Summary

In this chapter, we discussed how to internationalize a web page in Opa. We can either use the internal approach of writing a translate function in our code, or the external approach of utilizing an external file that is translated separately from our code.

Building a Chat Application

9

We have gone through the basic concepts of Opa and now it's time to build a real web application. In this chapter we will build a chat application. The application offers one chat room. The users who connect to the application will join the chat room automatically and can start discussing immediately. For simplicity, we supply a random username when a user joins. The source code for this application can be found at `https://github.com/winbomb/opapackt`.

The following is a screenshot of our chat application:

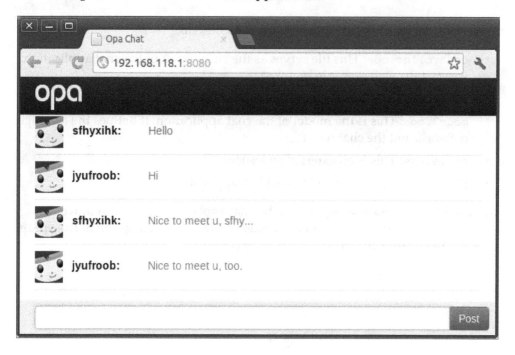

Creating a project

To begin developing our chat application, we need to create an Opa project using the following Opa command:

```
opa create chat
```

This command will create an empty Opa project. Also, it will generate the required directories and files automatically with the structure as shown in the following screenshot:

Let's have a brief look at what these source code files do:

- `controller.opa`: This file serves as the entry point of the chat application; we start the web server in `controller.opa`

- `view.opa`: This file serves as an user interface

- `model.opa`: This is the model of the chat application; it defines the message, network, and the chat room

- `style.css`: This is an external stylesheet file

- `Makefile`: This file is used to build an application

As we do not need database support in the chat application, we can remove `--import-package stdlib.database.mongo` from the FLAG option in `Makefile`. Type `make` and `make run` to run the empty application.

Launching the web server

Let's begin with `controller.opa`, the entry point of our chat application where we launch the web server. We have already discussed the function `Server.start` in the *Server module* section of *Chapter 3, Developing Web Applications*. In our chat application, we will use a handlers group to handle users requests.

```
Server.start(Server.http, [
    {resources: @static_resource_directory("resources")},
    {register: [{css:["/resources/css/style.css"]}]},
    {title:"Opa Chat", page: View.page }
])
```

So, what exactly are the arguments that we are passing to the `Server.start` function?

The line `{resources: @static_resource_direcotry("resources")}` registers a resource handler and will serve resource files in the `resources` directory.

Next, the line `{register: [{css:["/resources/css/style.css"]}]}` registers an external CSS file—`style.css`. This permits us to use styles in the `style.css` application scope.

Finally, the line `{title:"Opa Chat", page: View.page}` registers a single page handler that will dispatch all other requests to the function `View.page`.

The server uses the default configuration `Server.http` and will run on port 8080.

Designing user interface

When the application starts, all the requests (except requests for resources) will be distributed to the function `View.page`, which displays the chat page on the browser. Let's take a look at the view part; we define a module named `View` in `view.opa`.

```
import stdlib.themes.bootstrap.css
module View {
  function page(){
    user = Random.string(8)
    <div id=#title class="navbar navbar-inverse navbar-fixed-top">
      <div class=navbar-inner>
        <div id=#logo />
      </div>
    </div>
    <div id=#conversation class=container-fluid
      onready={function(_){Model.join(updatemsg)}} />
```

```
      <div id=#footer class="navbar navbar-fixed-bottom">
        <div class=input-append>
          <input type=text id=#entry class=input-xxlarge
            onnewline={broadcast(user)}/>
          <button class="btn btn-primary"
            onclick={broadcast(user)}>Post</button>
        </div>
      </div>
    }
    ...
  }
```

The module `View` contains functions to display the page on the browser. In the first line, `import stdlib.themes.bootstrap.css`, we import Bootstrap styles.

This permits us to use Bootstrap markup in our code, such as `navbar`, `navbar-fix-top`, and `btn-primary`. We also registered an external `style.css` file so we can use styles in `style.css` such as `conversation` and `footer`.

As we can see, this code in the function page follows almost the same syntax as HTML. As discussed in the *XHTML* section of *Chapter 3, Developing Web Applications*, we can use HTML freely in the Opa code, the HTML values having a predefined type `xhtml` in Opa.

Building application logic

A chat application is all about exchanging messages between users, so we need to define a message type. We can find its definition in the first line of `model.opa`:

```
type message = {string user, string text}
```

It's a very simple type with two fields. The `user` field represents the author of the message, and the `text` field represents the content of the message.

Now that we have the definition of a message, we need a way to pass the messages between different clients. As mentioned in *Chapter 5, Communicating between Client and Server*, Opa provides three ways for communicating between clients and servers: session, cell, and network. Session is for one-way asynchronous communication; cell is a special case of session and is for two-way synchronous communication; and network is for broadcasting messages to all observers. Network is the right choice for our purpose:

```
server private Network.network(message) room = Network.empty();
```

This code fragment defines an empty network named `room`. The type of the network is `Network.network(message)`, which means it is a network used to transmit data of the type `message`. The keyword `private` indicates that it cannot be accessed from other modules and the keyword `server` instructs Opa to implement this network on the server and not on the client.

We could also have used `Network.cloud(key)` to create a clouded network. This type of network will be automatically shared between multiple servers if the application is executed with the `cloud` option (for example, `./chat.js --cloud`). When one or several servers invoke `Network.cloud(key)` with the same value key, only one network is actually created on one of the participating servers (chosen arbitrarily), and the network will be shared between servers.

Now that we have our network, the next step is to add the clients to our network and broadcast messages to the clients. Therefore, we need two new functions:

```
function register(callback) {
  Network.add_callback(callback,room);
}
@async function broadcast(message) {
  Network.broadcast(message, room);
}
```

The function `register` registers a callback function to a given network. This registered function will be invoked whenever a new message arrives.

The function `broadcast` broadcasts messages to all the clients belonging to a given network. Note that the order in which clients receive the message is unspecified.

The complete code of `model.opa` is as follows:

```
type message = {string user, string text}
module Model {
  server private Network.network(message) room = Network.empty();
  @async function broadcast(message) {
    Network.broadcast(message, room);
  }
  function register(callback) {
    Network.add_callback(callback,room);
  }
}
```

Broadcasting and receiving messages

What is left for us to do is to connect the model and the view. There are two distinct functions that we need to accomplish.

We must broadcast the current user's message when the **Post** button is clicked on or when *Enter* is pressed in the text field. We must also display new messages as they arrive.

Let's first have a look at how we broadcast the user's message when they press *Enter*:

```
<button class="btn btn-primary"
onclick={broadcast(user)}>Post</button>
...
function broadcast(user)(_){
  text = Dom.get_value(#entry);
  Model.broadcast(~{user, text});
  Dom.clear_value(#entry);
}
```

When the user presses *Enter*, the `broadcast` function will be invoked. In this function, we first get the user's input using `Dom.get_value`, and then we broadcast the message in the second line by calling the `broadcast` method in the module `Model`. Finally, we clear the content of the input field. That's all it takes to broadcast the message to all the connected clients. Now let's review how we process new message arrivals. We have already mentioned the function `Model.register` in `model.opa`. Recall that it registers a callback function to the network. Consider the following code found in `view.opa`:

```
<div id=#conversation class=container-fluid
  onready={function(_){Model.register(updatemsg)}} />
```

When the div `#conversation` is ready, it invokes `Model.register` to register the callback function `updatemsg`, which will be called whenever a new message arrives:

```
function updatemsg(msg){
  line = <div class="row-fluid line">
          <div class="span1 userpic" />
          <div class="span2 user">{msg.user}:</>
          <div class="span9 message">{msg.text}</>
         </div>;
  #conversation =+ line;
  Dom.scroll_to_bottom(#conversation);
}
```

In the function `updatemsg`, we first construct an HTML fragment representing the message we have received. Then, we append a line to the end of the `Dom` element with the id `conversation`. Note that we are using the shortcut syntax `=+`. Finally, we use the function `Dom.scroll_to_bottom` to scroll the content to the bottom.

Summary

In this chapter, we have built a real web application in Opa. The application uses concepts and methods we have discussed in the previous chapters. First, we reviewed how to create an Opa project and how to start the web server. Then, we used the Bootstrap markup and customized styles to build the chat page in the module `View`.

Subsequently, we defined the chat message and the chat room in the module `Model`. Finally, we put them together to create the chat application.

10
Building a Game – Pacman

In this chapter, we will build the game called **Pacman**. We will learn how to program with the help of HTML5 Canvas in Opa, including drawing shapes, texts, and images on the canvas. We will also discuss how to use an external JavaScript library. The complete source code can be found at `https://github.com/winbomb/opapackt/tree/master/opacman`. Following is a screenshot of our Pacman game:

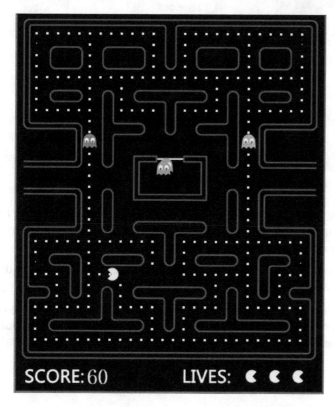

The project structure

Create an empty Opa project with the `opa create opacman` command. We need to modify the project structure. Let's first have a look at the modified project structure of our Pacman game:

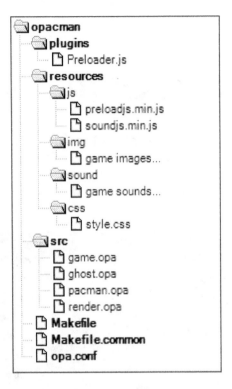

The following is a brief description of the project files:

- `src`: The source code, `ghost.opa` and `pacman.opa` define the type of ghost and Pacman, `render.opa` takes charge of drawing on the canvas, and `game.opa` contains the game logic

- `resources`: This folder contains the required resources, including images, sounds, and styles

- `resources/js`: `Preloadjs.min.js` and `soundjs.min.js` are two open source JavaScript libraries and are used to preload game resources and to play sounds

- plugins: Preloader.js is a plugin that we write to load game resources.

- We need to rewrite the opa.conf file to include the source code in the src directory:

  opacman.game has the following files:

    ◦ src/game.opa

    ◦ src/ghost.opa

    ◦ src/pacman.opa

    ◦ src/render.opa

We need to modify Makefile to remove database support as we do not need the database in this application. We also need to tell the compiler to compile the plugins with source code. These two jobs can be done by changing FLAG with the following line:

```
FLAG = --opx-dir _build $(PCKDIR)Preloader.js
```

The HTML5 Canvas

First of all, we need a canvas element on which to draw our graphics. The HTML5 Canvas element is an HTML tag similar to the <div>, <a>, and <table> tags, with the exception that its contents are rendered with JavaScript. In Opa, we create a canvas element the exact same way in which we create other HTML elements:

```
function page(){
    <canvas id=#gamecanvas width="520" height="620"
onready={Game.gamestart}>
</canvas>
}
```

This code creates a canvas with the gamecanvas ID. When the canvas element is ready, the Game.gamestart function will be invoked to start the game.

Next we must get the canvas context. It is important for us to understand the difference between the canvas element and the canvas context. The canvas element is a DOM node embedded in the HTML page, whereas the canvas context is an object with properties and methods that you can use to render graphics inside the canvas element. The context can be 2D or 3D (WebGL). In our Pacman game, we are using the 2D context. To get the canvas 2D context, we use the Canvas.get_context_2d function. The following code fragment demonstrates how to get the canvas context for a given ID:

```
ctx = match(Canvas.get(#gamecanvas)){
case {none}: {none}
```

```
case ~{some}: Canvas.get_context_2d(some)
}
```

Note that each canvas element can only have one context. If we use the `Canvas.get_context_2d` method multiple times for the same element, it will return the same context.

Drawing a shape

Now that we have the context of our canvas element, we can draw graphics on it. Opa and JavaScript use similar code to draw the graphics. The primary difference between them is that the drawing functions in Opa are static. All drawing methods can be found in the `Canvas` module.

Using the fill and stroke properties

Whenever we wish to draw shapes on a canvas, there are two properties that we need to set: `Stroke` and `Fill`. `Stroke` and `fill` determine how the shape is drawn. The `stroke` property is used for the outline of a shape; the `fill` property is used for the inside of a shape. In the following example, the first two lines fill a rectangle, whereas the last three lines stroke a rectangle:

```
Canvas.save(ctx)
Canvas.set_fill_style(ctx,{color: Color.red})
Canvas.fill_rect(ctx,10,10,100,50)
Canvas.set_stroke_style(ctx,{color: Color.black})
Canvas.set_line_width(ctx,5.0)
Canvas.stroke_rect(ctx,120,10,100,50)
Canvas.restore(ctx)
```

Following is the result of the preceding code fragment:

Note that we used `Canvas.save` and `Canvas.restore` in the preceding code. Each canvas context maintains a stack of drawing states such as `fillStyle` and `strokeStyel`. Since a canvas can only have one 2D context, `Canvas.save` and `Canvas.restore` are used to save and restore canvas states in short.

Drawing a curve

In our game, we create our Pacman by drawing an arc on the canvas. When the Pacman's mouth is open, we draw a pie, and when it's closed, we draw a circle.

We can draw the pie and the circle both with the `Canvas.arc` function. Arcs are defined by a center point, a radius, a starting angle, an ending angle, and the drawing direction (either clockwise or counterclockwise). The following diagram shows how we should draw the Pacman when he is facing left:

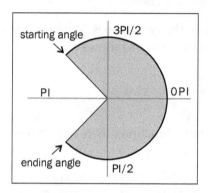

First, we move to the center point and begin drawing from the starting angle `5*PI/4`. We then draw an arc to the ending angle `3*PI/4` moving clockwise. Finally, we fill and stroke the shape. Here is the code:

```
Canvas.set_stroke_style(ctx,{color:Color.black})
Canvas.set_fill_style(ctx,{color:Color.yellow})
Canvas.begin_path(ctx)
Canvas.move_to(ctx,100,100)
Canvas.arc(ctx,100,100,50,5.0*Math.PI/4.0,3.0*Math.PI/4.0,{false})
Canvas.close_path(ctx)
Canvas.fill(ctx)
Canvas.stroke(ctx)
```

Drawing an image

To display an image on HTML5 Canvas in Opa, we can use the `Canvas.draw_image` function that requires an image object and a destination point. Since the `draw_image` method requires an image object, we must first create an image and wait for it to load before we can draw it on the canvas. In our game, we will preload all images and sounds at the beginning of the game as you will see later. The `Canvas.draw_image` function is declared as follows:

```
void draw_image(Canvas.context ctx, Canvas.image img, int x, int y)
```

The first argument that we pass to `draw_image` is the canvas context that we retrieved. The second argument is the image object of type `Canvas.image`. The `Canvas.image` type is declared as:

```
type Canvas.image = {Image.image    image}
                 or {Canvas.canvas canvas}
                 or {Video.video    video}
```

`Image.image` is an external type. It is identical to the image type that we created in JavaScript with the `new Image()` code.

We preload the images when the game starts. When needed, we will obtain an image object by calling the plugin function as follows:

```
function IMAGE(key){
    {image: %%Preloader.get%%(key)}
}
```

In addition to the draw_image function, there are two more functions that we can use to draw images on canvas:

```
Canvas.draw_image_with_dimensions(ctx, img, x, y, w, h)
Canvas.draw_image_full(ctx, img, sx, sy, sw, sh, dx, dy, dw, dh)
```

To set the size of an image, we can use `draw_image_with_dimensions`. This will scale the image to the target size. The `draw_image_full` function is even more powerful, as we can use it to crop the image.

Drawing the text

To display texts on a canvas in Opa, we can use the `Canvas.fill_text` or `Canvas.stroke_text` method. We can change the fill style or stroke style by invoking `Canvas.set_fill_style` or `Canvas.set_stroke_style` respectively.

To set the font of the text, use the `Canvas.set_font` function. We should pass the font information to the method; the font information is a string matching the following pattern:

```
[font-style] [font-weight] [font-size] [font-family]
```

The following code draws the word "start" twice, one is filled and the other is stroked, both with font information `italic bold 40px verdana`:

```
Canvas.set_fill_style(ctx,{color:Color.red})
Canvas.set_font(ctx,"italic bold 40px verdana")
Canvas.fill_text(ctx,"Start",5,50)
```

```
Canvas.set_stroke_style(ctx,{color:Color.red})
Canvas.set_line_width(ctx,2.0)
Canvas.stroke_text(ctx,"Start",200,50)
```

The result of the preceding code fragment is as follows:

Binding the external JavaScript library

In our Pacman game, we need to preload game resources such as images and sounds. We need to play sounds and music as well. Of course, we could write our own code to accomplish these tasks. However, why reinvent the wheel? There are numerous JavaScript libraries that make our job easier. The following section shows how to bind an existing JavaScript library into our game.

Preloading the resources

When a program requires multiple images and sounds, as is the case with our Pacman game, it's usually a good idea to load all of the resources before displaying or playing them. There are many excellent JavaScript libraries available. For our purposes, the Preload JS 0.3.0 (for resource) and SoundJS 0.4.0 (for sounds) libraries are a good fit. You can download Preload JS 0.3.0 from `https://github.com/CreateJS/PreloadJS` and the SoundJS 0.4.0 library is available at `https://github.com/CreateJS/SoundJS`.

To bind the JavaScript library, we must register those functions that we plan to call from within our Opa code. We have discussed how to bind JavaScript in *Chapter 6, Binding with Other Languages*. In our Pacman game, we register a `preload` function:

```
/** @register {( -> void) -> void} */
function preload(callback) {
    //use LoadQueue to preload resources, invoke callback when finish.
    queue = new createjs.LoadQueue();
    queue.installPlugin(createjs.Sound);
    queue.addEventListener("complete", callback);
    queue.loadManifest([ ... ])
}
```

The `preload` function uses `PreloadJS` to preload resources, and will invoke a callback when it is finished. We can call the `preload` function in Opa in the following way:

```
%%Preloader.preload%%(function(){
    //start our game after resources have been loaded.
})
```

The complete code can be found in `plugins/preloader.js` and `/src/game.opa`.

Playing sounds

We bind the `SoundJS` library and play sounds by registering a function in the `preloader.js` plugin file. The function invokes methods from SoundJS to build a sound instance and then play it. The `SoundJS` library is entirely out of the scope of this book. For more details regarding the use of this library visit the SoundJS homepage.

Summary

In this chapter, we built a game called **Pacman**. First, we discussed how to declare an HTML5 Canvas element and how to get canvas context. Then, we reviewed how to draw shapes, images, and texts on a canvas. Finally, we showed how to write a plugin and embed external JavaScript libraries in the application.

11
Developing a Social Mobile Application – LiveRoom

In this chapter, we will build a social mobile web application that we call LiveRoom. LiveRoom offers functionality similar to a forum. Users can login and post discussions and messages; they can also sign in with their Facebook account. The application will be able to support both mobile devices and desktop browsers. The following is a screenshot of LiveRoom and the source code is available at https://github.com/winbomb/opapackt/tree/master/liveroom

Project structure

First, let's have a look at the project structure. It's a classical Opa project structure; we can create a similar structure with the following command line:

```
opa create liveroom
```

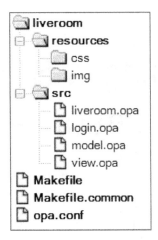

- `liveroom.opa`: The entry point of the application. It declares the database, dispatches the requests, and starts the web server.

- `login.opa`: The login module. It shows the login page, handles the `UserContext` when the user logs in and logs out, and connects to Facebook when the user tries to sign in with Facebook.

- `model.opa`: The data model of the application. It defines data models and deals with database reading and writing.

- `view.opa`: The UI (user interface). It shows the pages, maps what we fetch from the database into XHTML, and then shows them on the page. And moreover, it gets the user's input and tries to insert data into the database through the `Model` module.

- `style.css`: The external style sheet. It's registered when the web server starts, so we can use styles in this file application scope.

To compile and run the application, type `make run`.

Authorizing a user

In this section, we will discuss how to make a simple sign in and sign out system that is an essential part of this forum and a subset of functionality that is frequently needed for other types of websites as well.

Signing in and signing out

For simplicity, we do not provide a sign up process for the application. Users who input a non-blank username and password can log in to the system. `Model.auth` returns {none} if authorization fails, otherwise it returns {user}, where user is a value of type `User.t` containing information about the current user. Only signed in users will be able to create topics and post messages. This section will show you what you should do when users sign in. The following code fragment demonstrates the sign in, the code can be found in the `login.opa` file:

```
type Login.user = {unlogged} or {User.t user}
state = UserContext.make(Login.user {unlogged})
function login(_) {
username = Dom.get_value(#username)
  password = Dom.get_value(#password)
  match(Model.auth(username,password)){
  case {none}: Client.reload()
  case {some:user}: {
      UserContext.change(function(_){~{user}},state)
          Client.goto("/")
  }}
}
```

The type `Login.user` is a sum type: {unlogged} means the current user has not signed in; {Usert.t user} means the current user has signed in and user information is stored in this record. As we can see from the second line, `UserContext` is used to manage the login state. `UserContext` is a high-level mechanism based on cookies. It is used to associate values with each client. The user's data stored in `UserContext` can only be accessed and modified by the user who owns this data. For most of our needs, we only need to use the following functions supplied by `UserContext`.

Use the `UserContext.make` function to create a `UserContext` with a default value; this is what we do in the second line.

Use the `UserContext.change` function to change the current state of the `UserContext` for this user. Note that in line nine of the previous code, we changed the state to ~{user} after a successful authorization.

Use the `UserContext.remove` function to remove the current value. The following code removes the value when a user signs out:

```
function logout(_){
UserContext.remove(state)
  Client.reload()
}
```

Use the `UserContext.get` function to get the current value of the `UserContext`. The following code uses this function to get the name of the current signed in user:

```
function get_user() {
  match(UserContext.get(state)){
    case {unlogged}: "anonymous"
    case ~{user}:    user.nickname
  }
}
```

This is how we can implement a default user login. However, we can also allow the user to finish signing in with his or her Facebook or Twitter account.

Signing in with Facebook

Opa provides the modules FbAuth and Twitter to connect with Facebook and Twitter respectively. In the login page of LiveRoom, there is a link button that allows the user to sign in with Facebook. There are some additional steps required to authenticate with Facebook, and it is beyond the scope of this book to go into all the details of authenticating with Facebook, since we instead want to focus on the Opa language. Those who would like to know more about Facebook authentication should review the following excellent tutorial: `https://github.com/akoprow/opa-devcamp-facebook`.

Note that you should replace the x's in `login.opa` with your real data:

```
config = {
app_id: "xxxxxxxxxxxxxxxx",
api_key: "xxxxxxxxxxxxxxx",
app_secret: "xxxxxxxxxxxxxxxxxxxxxxxxxxxxxx"
}
```

`App_id` and `app_key` are identical, and `app_secret` should not be shared with anyone.

The application

LiveRoom is all about posting topics and messages. When users sign in, they can start discussions by creating new topics. The newly created topics will be shown in the list of most recent discussions, namely the latest discussions list. If a user clicks on a topic, he/she will enter the discussion and get a list of messages related to the topic. If he/she has signed in, he/she will be able to post a message related to the topic that he/she selected, or comment on an existing message. The following figure shows the data model of topic, message, and comment:

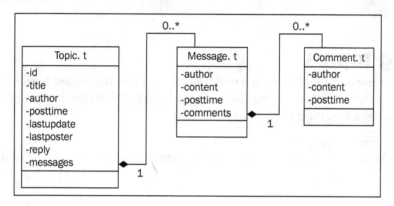

And here are the type definitions in Opa:

```
type Topic.t = {
   int    id,     //id, the primary key
   string title,     //title of the topic
   string author,   //the author
   int    posttime,   //post time
   int    lastupdate,   //last update time,
   string lastposter,  //last poster
   int    reply,     //number of replies
   stringmap(Message.t) messages
}
type Message.t = {
string author, string content, int posttime,
   list(Comment.t) comments
}
type Comment.t = { string author, string content, int posttime }
```

With these data model definitions in place, we can declare our database `liveroom`:

```
database liveroom {
   int     /next_id
   Topic.t /topics[{id}]
}
```

The database path `next_id` is an integer holding the max topic id; this is a solution to simulate an auto-increment key that MongoDB does not natively support. The `topics` path stores the topics that the users users create. The primary key is the topic's id.

Listing topics

On the main page of LiveRoom, we will display recently discussed topics that were fetched from the database. In Opa this is an easy task. The following function query retrieves a specified page of topics:

```
function query(page){
   topics = /liveroom/topics[skip page*50;limit 50;order -lastupdate]
   DbSet.iterator(topics)
}
```

Really simple, isn't it? As we have discussed in *Chapter 7, Working with Databases,* we can read data from the database by using a database path such as `/liveroom/topics`. The statements in square brackets are querying conditions. The query result `topics` is a dbset, we convert it into iteration in the next line, so we can loop the result in the following way:

```
Iter.map(function(t){
... //map a topic to an xhtml showing on the page
}, query(0))
```

This is exactly what we do in the user interface code. Please refer to `list_topics` in the module View for details. To list messages and comments, you will also need to use similar code. First, we fetch a topic from the database for a given id:

```
function get(id) {
/liveroom/topics[~{id}]
}
```

We then iterate on messages and comments in the module View to convert them into XHTML and display them on the page. The code is as follows:

```
topic = Model.get(id)
Map.iter(function(key, msg){
    ...
  List.map(function(comment){
     ...
  }, msg.comments)
}, topic.messages)
```

Check the function `show_messages` in the module View for the complete code.

Creating a topic

One of the most important use cases of LiveRoom is creating a topic. When users have signed in, they will be able to create a topic by clicking on **new topic** on the main page. This will navigate users to a topic creating page where they can input the title and content. When users click on the **create** button, the function `add_topic` will be invoked:

```
function add_topic(_){L
   topic = ...   //create a topic record from user's input
match(Model.insert(topic)){  //insert the record into database
    case {success: _}: Client.goto("/")   //go back to main page
    case {failure: f}: show_alert("{f}")   //show alert info
  }
}
```

The `add_topic` function first creates a record of type `Topic.t` from the user's input. It then tries to insert the topic into the database by calling the `Model.insert` function defined as follows:

```
function insert(topic){
  match(next_id()){
  case {none}: {failure: "Failed to generate next id!"}
  case {some:id}:{
    /liveroom/topics[~{id}] <- {topic with ~id}
    {success: id}
  }}
}
```

Because there is no auto-increment id in MongoDB, we use the `next_id` function to get a unique identifier. The function returns {none} if it fails, otherwise it returns `some(id)`, where `id` is the next identifier. In the `next_id` function, we use the Mongo API `MongoCommands.findAndUpdateOpa` to perform an atomic operation:

```
my_db = MongoConnection.openfatal("default")
function next_id(){
  if(?/liveroom/next_id == none) { /liveroom/next_id <- 0 }
    r = MongoCommands.findAndUpdateOpa(
        my_db, "liveroom", "_default",
        Bson.opa2doc({_id : "/liveroom/next_id"}),
        Bson.opa2doc({`$inc` : { value : 1}}),
{some : true}, {none}
  );
  match (r) {
    case { success : {string _id, int value} v }: some(v.value)
    case { failure : e }: {none}
}
}
```

Posting messages and comments

As we can tell from the data type `Topic.t` that we use to store messages in a string map inside a topic, we need a string key to access or update a message. In LiveRoom, we use {topic id}_{system time}_{random string} as a key. After inserting a message, some other fields, such as reply, need to be updated too.

```
function post_message(id, message){
  now = get_now()   //current time in milliseconds
  key = "{id}_{now}_{Random.string(5)}"
  /liveroom/topics[~{id}]/messages[key] <- message
  /liveroom/topics[~{id}]/reply++
  /liveroom/topics[~{id}]/lastupdate = now
  /liveroom/topics[~{id}]/lastposter = message.author
}
```

To post a comment, just append a new item to the list of comments for a given topic id and the message key:

```
function post_comment(id, key, comment){
  /liveroom/topics[~{id}]/messages[key]/comments <+ comment
}
```

Designing for mobile devices

To make sure whether our LiveRoom application is supported on mobile devices, we have to do a little more work. A viewport metatag needs to be put into the `<head>` tag of the page:

```
header = <><meta name="viewport" content="width=device-width,
initial-scale=1.0, user-scalable=no"></>
xhtml = <>...</> //the body of the page
Resource.full_page("Live Room", xhtml, header, {success}, [])
```

Here we use `Resource.full_page` to embed the `viewport` meta tag into our page. A detailed description of this function can be found online (`http://doc.opalang.org`).

Next, we need to import `bootstrap.responsive` to help our application to be more responsive.

```
import stdlib.themes.{bootstrap, bootstrap.responsive}
```

You can find more information about responsive Bootstrap classes on the Bootstrap home page: `http://twitter.github.io/bootstrap/scaffolding.html#responsive`

In our LiveRoom application, we use the responsive Bootstrap class `hide-phone` to hide the column `last poster` on mobile phones when listing the topics as there may not be enough width. The following code shows how we can do that:

```
<td align="center" class="hidden-phone">{t.lastposter}</td>
...
<th align="center" class="hidden-phone">Last Poster</th>
```

We can find the code in the function `main` of `view.opa`.

Summary

In this chapter, we described how to write a social mobile web application in Opa. First, we talked about the user authorization procedure; we used `UserContext` to maintain the login state for a given client. We also mentioned how to connect with Facebook in Opa. In the next section, we discussed in detail how to implement LiveRoom, this included reading data from the database and displaying it in the webpage, and inserting user submitted topics, messages, and comments into the database. Please refer to the source code to review the complete code.

Index

Thank you for buying
Opa Application Development

About Packt Publishing

Packt, pronounced 'packed', published its first book *"Mastering phpMyAdmin for Effective MySQL Management"* in April 2004 and subsequently continued to specialize in publishing highly focused books on specific technologies and solutions.

Our books and publications share the experiences of your fellow IT professionals in adapting and customizing today's systems, applications, and frameworks. Our solution based books give you the knowledge and power to customize the software and technologies you're using to get the job done. Packt books are more specific and less general than the IT books you have seen in the past. Our unique business model allows us to bring you more focused information, giving you more of what you need to know, and less of what you don't.

Packt is a modern, yet unique publishing company, which focuses on producing quality, cutting-edge books for communities of developers, administrators, and newbies alike. For more information, please visit our website: www.packtpub.com.

About Packt Open Source

In 2010, Packt launched two new brands, Packt Open Source and Packt Enterprise, in order to continue its focus on specialization. This book is part of the Packt Open Source brand, home to books published on software built around Open Source licences, and offering information to anybody from advanced developers to budding web designers. The Open Source brand also runs Packt's Open Source Royalty Scheme, by which Packt gives a royalty to each Open Source project about whose software a book is sold.

Writing for Packt

We welcome all inquiries from people who are interested in authoring. Book proposals should be sent to author@packtpub.com. If your book idea is still at an early stage and you would like to discuss it first before writing a formal book proposal, contact us; one of our commissioning editors will get in touch with you.

We're not just looking for published authors; if you have strong technical skills but no writing experience, our experienced editors can help you develop a writing career, or simply get some additional reward for your expertise.

Ext JS 4 First Look

ISBN: 978-1-84951-666-2   Paperback: 340 pages

A practical guide including examples of the new features in Ext JS 4 and tips to migrate from Ext JS 3

1. Migrate your Ext JS 3 applications easily to Ext JS 4 based on the examples presented in this guide

2. Full of diagrams, illustrations, and step-by-step instructions to develop real word applications

3. Driven by examples and explanations of how things work

Sencha Touch Mobile JavaScript Framework

ISBN: 978-1-84951-510-8   Paperback: 316 pages

Build web applications for Apple iOS and Google Android touchscreen devices with this first HTML5 mobile framework

1. Learn to develop web applications that look and feel native on Apple iOS and Google Android touchscreen devices using Sencha Touch through examples

2. Design resolution-independent and graphical representations like buttons, icons, and tabs of unparalleled flexibility

3. Add custom events like tap, double tap, swipe, tap and hold, pinch, and rotate

Please check **www.PacktPub.com** for information on our titles